THE ACCESS CURRICULUM

Intentional, Integrated and Inquiry-based
For Ages Infancy through Grade Five

Shauna M. Adams, Ed.D.,
Joni L. Baldwin, Ed.D.,
Joy L. Comingore, M.A.,
Mary Kay Kelly, Ph.D.

THE ACCESS CURRICULUM

Intentional, Integrated and Inquiry-based
For Ages Infancy through Grade Five

Shauna M. Adams, Ed.D.,
Joni L. Baldwin, Ed.D.,
Joy L. Comingore, M.A.,
Mary Kay Kelly, Ph.D.

Credits
Infant and Toddler implications contributed by Becky Anderson, M.S.Ed.
Edited by Rebecca Aicher, M.A.
Cover Design: Meredith A. Adams, B.F.A.
Photographs taken at the Bombeck Family Learning Center
by Jessica R. Pike, M.S.Ed. and Meredith A. Adams, B.F.A.

This book was printed in the United States of America.

Rev. date: 09/20/2013

To order additional copies of this book, contact:
Xlibris LLC
1-888-795-4274
www.Xlibris.com
Orders@Xlibris.com
110325

Contents

Dedication

This book is dedicated to Dr. Thomas Lasley. Without his vision and support, there would be no Bombeck Family Learning Center. Although he humbly professed limited knowledge of early childhood education, he has spent much of his career championing the cause so that someday every young person in the Dayton region will be ready to learn by kindergarten and ready to earn by graduation.

Acknowledgements

First and foremost we would like to thank the teachers, staff, children and families of the University of Dayton Bombeck Family Learning Center. They inspire our work each and every day.

We would also like to acknowledge our own families who have supported our work in so many ways.

Preface

The *ACCESS* Curriculum is an intentional, integrated and inquiry-based curriculum for children ages infancy through grade five. It was developed at the University of Dayton Bombeck Family Learning Center by teachers, administrators, the curriculum specialist and early and middle childhood faculty. *ACCESS* has been piloted in a variety of early care and education settings and also in public, Catholic, and charter schools in grades preschool through 3 and aspects of the curriculum can also be applied to middle school classrooms. The curriculum was developed out of respect for the intelligence and creativity of teachers who seek to create cohesive, engaging and meaningful curriculum. It also embraces children as capable thinkers who have important questions to be answered.

ACCESS is a research-based curriculum that reflects the position statements of the National Association for the Education of Young Children (NAEYC) (2009) and the Division of Early Childhood of the Council for Exceptional Children (DEC) (Sandall, Hemmeter, Smith & McLean, 2005) as well as the Association for Middle Level Education (AMLE) which states that "adolescents must become actively aware of the larger world, asking significant and relevant questions about that world and wrestling with big ideas and questions for which there may not be one right answer" (2010, p.1).

ACCESS can incorporate a variety of content standards including the Common Core State Standards and others adopted by individual states like *Ohio's Early Learning and Development Standards* (Ohio Department of Education, 2012) for young children birth through 5. The *Head Start Child Development and Early Learning Framework* (Head Start Resource Center, 2010) can easily be used with *ACCESS* as can courses of study developed by Catholic Dioceses. Nontraditional educational programs such as nature centers, museums, and community center programs also find that *ACCESS* is appropriate. *ACCESS* can be used in conjunction with other curriculum or can stand alone.

We believe that effective teachers must be able not only to create appropriate integrated and inquiry-based curriculum, but also to articulate their practice to parents, administrators, board members, policy makers and other stakeholders who may lack an understanding of appropriate and effective curriculum and assessments. To this end, each chapter provides a review of the research that supports the elements outlined in each chapter.

ACCESS is an acronym designed to organize the elements in a structure that is easy to remember. *ACCESS* stands for:

> **A**ssessment-Supported
> **C**hild-
> **C**entered
> **E**mergent-Negotiated
> **S**cience Emphasis
> **S**tandards Integrated

This book begins with Chapter 1 which is an overview of the *ACCESS* Curriculum. Chapters 2-6 represent the elements of the acronym as follows: Assessment-Supported; Child-Centered; Emergent-Negotiated; Science Emphasis; and Standards Integrated. Each chapter begins by providing the research-base needed for teachers to articulate their practice and includes a description of implementation with infants and toddlers, preschooler and elementary grades students. A section entitled, "*ACCESS* Steps for Success" is near the end of each chapter and provides a quick reference for teachers as they implement *ACCESS*. An inclusive reference section gives credit to the extensive research-base that informs the *ACCESS* Curriculum. Methods for including families are embedded throughout the book. *ACCESS* is designed to be used with all children including those with exceptionalities. Many prekindergarten special needs teachers have adopted *ACCESS*. Chapter 7, Including Children with Exceptionalities, was written to provide special educators with additional information on how to adapt and modify curriculum, differentiate curriculum, and address IEP or IFSP goals.

Finally, *ACCESS* is supported by a dynamic website, *www.accesscurriculum. com*, which includes many examples of practice both at the Bombeck Family Learning Center and in other classrooms that have adopted *ACCESS*. Of particular interest to those who are adopting *ACCESS* should be the *ACCESS* Collection which includes forms, assessment tools, and other exciting resources including the web-based Science Concept Planner. The *ACCESS* Curriculum website in general and the *ACCESS* collection more specifically provide *ACCESS* users with the tools and inspiration that lead to successful implementation.

References

Association for Middle Level Educators. (2010). *This we believe: Keys to educating young adolescents.* Westerville, OH: Author.

Head Start Resource Center. (2010). *The Head Start child development and early learning framework promoting positive outcomes in early childhood programs serving children 3-5 years old.* Arlington, VA: Office of Head Start, Administration for Children and Families, U.S. Department of Health and Human Services.

National Association for the Education of Young Children. (2009). *Developmentally appropriate practice in early childhood programs serving children from birth through age 8.* Washington DC: Author.

Ohio Department of Education. (2012). *Ohio's early learning and development standards.* Columbus, OH: Author.

Sandall, S., Hemmeter, M.L., Smith B.J., & McLean, M.E. (EDs.). (2005). *DEC recommended practices: A comprehensive guide for practical application in early intervention/early childhood special education.* Missoula, MT: Division for Early Childhood.

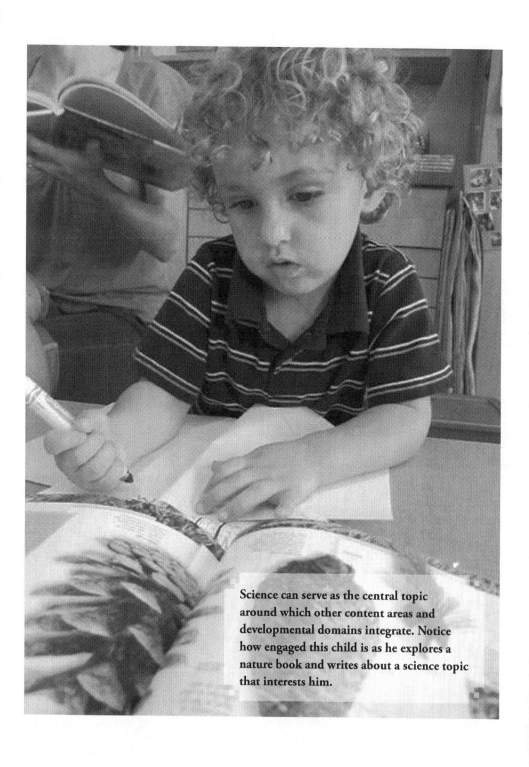

Science can serve as the central topic around which other content areas and developmental domains integrate. Notice how engaged this child is as he explores a nature book and writes about a science topic that interests him.

1

The ACCESS Curriculum: An Overview

- *Childhood is a unique and valuable stage of the human life cycle. Our paramount responsibility is to provide care and education in settings that are safe, healthy, nurturing, and responsive for each child (National Association for the Education of Young Children, 2005, p. 2).*
- *When we instruct children in academic subjects . . . at too early an age, we miseducate them; we put them at risk for short-term stress and long-term personality damage for no useful purpose. There is no evidence that such early instruction has lasting benefits, and [there is] considerable evidence that it can do lasting harm (Elkind, 1987, p. 3).*
- *Backing off from high standards because they are hard to reach denies many (young) children the opportunity to learn and is the death knell for their future (Bowman, 2006, p. 48).*
- *Children are not innately ready or not ready for school. Their skills and development are strongly influenced by their families and through their interactions with other people and environments before coming to school (Maxwell & Clifford, 2004, p. 42).*

These voices represent early childhood's past, present and future and demonstrate the need to be intentional about how we, early childhood educators, provide access to quality, developmentally appropriate learning experiences for young children. The *ACCESS Curriculum (ACCESS)* was developed, in part, to fill that need. *ACCESS* is a curriculum that includes a framework for intentional decision-making about what to teach and how to teach it. It was developed and implemented at the University of Dayton's (UD) demonstration school, the Bombeck Family Learning Center (Bombeck Center) and with our field partners in other preschool, kindergarten and primary grade settings. The curriculum reflects 15 years of work by UD early childhood faculty and the Bombeck Center curriculum specialist, teachers and administrators who developed, field tested and implemented the curriculum.

ACCESS:

- uses ongoing program evaluation and assessment data about what children know and are able to do to support instructional decision-making;
- encourages high quality teacher-child interactions and is child centered;
- benefits from an emergent/negotiated curriculum component that incorporates integrated, extended investigations;
- provides children with opportunities to acquire both developmental skills and subject matter content appropriate for their age; and
- supports teacher development of in-depth content knowledge to support child learning outcomes.

ACCESS was developed as an approach to early childhood curriculum that supports intentional decision-making about what and how to teach young children, from birth through age 8, in the 21st century. The curriculum reflects respect for the intelligence of young children and their teachers who provide responsive care and quality educational experiences. While some in the field have developed curricula that steer away from the emergent, child-centered models that have been the theoretical foundation of early childhood, this curriculum embraces the traditions of the field while also pushing the professional forward to better serve children and families as they face the demands of the 21st century.

Play can provide a context for academic content. This young girl is predicting which shape of tube will support the most blocks. She needs to count and record the number of blocks to keep track of her findings. She discovers that trianglular shaped tubes provide the strongest supports.

ACCESS avoids the "either/or" view of early childhood curriculum that has the play-based traditionalist on one end of the developmentally appropriate practice continuum while reformists hover on the other end, embracing an academic emphasis on content standards. *ACCESS* is based on a "both/and" perspective that incorporates a rich, child-centered, emergent curriculum model. This model is supported by authentic assessment allowing teachers to make well-informed decisions about how to stage the learning environment, select engaging materials, and plan meaningful and connected experiences that allow young children to investigate important topics. The curriculum builds upon young children's natural curiosity about the world around them by fostering a sense of wonder and providing opportunities for scientific inquiry. It also capitalizes on the teachable moments that present themselves throughout the child's daily routines.

Based on the understanding that no single curriculum can meet the needs of all learners, (Frede & Ackerman, 2007), *ACCESS* describes a process for making informed decisions that reflects the needs of children and families in a variety of early care and educational settings including but not limited to child care, early intervention, Head Start and public and private schools that house preschool, preschool special education, kindergarten and the primary grades.

ACCESS integrates the study of important science topics with opportunities for language, social, emotional, physical health, motor, aesthetic, and cognitive development as well as meaningful literacy, math and social studies learning with an emphasis on approaches to learning and executive functions. It is appropriate for young children, ages birth to eight, including those who are typically developing, at-risk and those with mild to moderate learning needs. *ACCESS* has been field tested in a variety of settings including programs that serve children and families in poverty. In alignment with New's premise that "all children are entitled to gain access to the skills and knowledge regarded as social capital in the dominant culture" (1999, p. 132), early childhood professionals use *ACCESS* to push past curriculum models that support educational equity rather than sensitivity to differences. *ACCESS* sets the stage so that children with a variety of life experiences can **access** high quality, intellectually engaging curriculum. Because of an emphasis on academic language (Nagy & Townsend, 2011) and the inclusion of novel vocabulary, *ACCESS* adapts to the needs of children who are English language learners and native speakers alike. The *Intentional Curriculum Decision-Making Process* (Figure 1-1) that is the basis of *ACCESS*, allows teachers to make decisions that reflect the needs of diverse children and families including those who differ in terms of geographical location, cultural background, socio-economic status, race, religion, ethnicity and learning styles and abilities. The curriculum is flexible and can address any set of content standards including but not limited to the:

- *Common Core State Standards* (National Governors Association Center for Best Practices and the Council of Chief State School Officers, 2009),
- *Head Start Child Development and Early Learning Framework* (Head Start Resource Center, 2010),
- *K-12 Science Framework* (National Research Council, 2012),
- Early learning and development standards and infant/toddler guidelines adopted by individual states, and
- Graded courses of study adopted by public, charter, Catholic and other private schools.

ACCESS can be used in conjunction with other curricula, formal or informal, and can support the annual goals and instructional objectives on individual education plans.

Why ACCESS was Developed

Early childhood faculty, the Bombeck Center Curriculum Specialist and Bombeck Center teachers and administrators began to re-examine how instructional decisions were made when early learning content standards were first adopted by the State of Ohio in 2004. Prior to that time, the Bombeck Center identified itself as a center that demonstrated developmentally appropriate practice, incorporated the *Project Approach* (Katz & Chard, 2000) and focused on science. As early learning content standards became a more integral part of the Bombeck Center curriculum, it became apparent that the new standards both benefited and challenged the Bombeck Center program. As a benefit, the early learning content standards were developmentally appropriate and provided opportunities to be more systematic about the concepts and skills to which children were exposed. The sheer number of standards was overwhelming and difficult for teachers to track and to teach in meaningful, connected and child-directed ways. To add to the challenge, the standards overlapped across content areas creating redundancy.

In 2006, the Ohio Child Care Resource and Referral Agency, working in conjunction with the Ohio Department of Jobs and Family Services, released the *Ohio Infant and Toddler Guidelines*. These guidelines emphasized developmental skills for young children from birth through 36 months and addressed skills in the following domains: social, emotional, cognitive, language and communication, motor, and physical and health. These developmental guidelines serve as the basis for infant and toddler curriculum using *ACCESS* which can be adapted to include any set of standards or developmental guidelines.

ACCESS allows teachers to easily adapt to new content standards and/ or developmental guidelines because the curriculum relies on authentic assessment that can be adjusted when new content standards/statements or developmental guidelines are adopted. For example, in 2010, the *Common Core State Standards* were adopted by 45 states to represent what students in grades kindergarten through 12 should know and be able to do in the areas of literacy and math. Teachers using *ACCESS* reviewed the new content standards, compared them to prior standards and made adjustments to their authentic assessment system. Because the assessment system informs instruction, teachers learned the new content and incorporated it into their curriculum without having to completely revise their curriculum process. This same realignment process will take place when the National Research Council releases the final draft of the new science framework and content standards for grades kindergarten through 12 in 2013.

Quality Curriculum First, then Support with Assessment

ACCESS grew out of the Bombeck Center's commitment to an emergent/ negotiated, child-centered and science focused integrated curriculum that became more cohesive as the Bombeck Center's curriculum team developed a manageable assessment system. It quickly became apparent that assessment and documentation needed to be a stronger focus in the curriculum. Like many programs for young children, the curriculum team was faced with a difficult decision. To keep track of the complex and numerous content standards, the Bombeck Center needed to either adopt a commercial curriculum that was aligned with the state standards or develop a system for tracking what children know and are able to do. Our roots were grounded in an emergent/negotiated, play-based and child-centered curriculum model that incorporated extended investigations and followed the interests of the children. We also found that many of the commercial curricula on the market lacked depth in the area of science which was an important part of who we were. We were careful **not** to allow assessment data to drive instructional decisions as was becoming common in the field. Instead, we focused on important science concepts, created experiences that allowed children to investigate the concepts while teachers tracked naturally-occurring content standards and developmental skills.

Content Standards: Divide and Conquer

Like many effective early childhood educators, the Bombeck Center teaching staff was well grounded in their understanding of developmental skills. This knowledge was incorporated throughout the program. Teachers could call on their deep understanding of development and apply it automatically as they made instructional decisions throughout the day. In 2004, the teachers did not, however, have a deep or automatic understanding of the new content standards. One of our first tasks in the development of *ACCESS* was to divide the standards into manageable and easy to remember chunks of which the teachers could make sense. We also needed to make connections across content areas while reducing the redundancy that existed in the State standards.

While becoming familiar with the new document, the teachers noted that there were different kinds of standards. Some standards, especially in the areas of science and social studies, leant themselves to deep concept development most effectively addressed in the context of an extended investigation. The standards addressed during investigations were often documented through portfolio entries. Other standards were commonly addressed during daily activities and routines. Many of the standards in this category overlapped with developmental skills and were noted in interactions with families especially during parent conferences. Progress reports and ongoing communications with families were natural methods for documenting and communicating these standards.

Once teachers determined that they were already documenting many of the standards through existing strategies, they were much more comfortable with collecting assessment data for the remaining standards, many of which were categorized as skills that required more intentional assessment and record keeping. The teachers developed a series of informal data collection tools that they could choose from to reflect their personal teaching style. While data collection strategies were determined by the teacher, all teachers were expected to aggregate data on the *ACCESS Class Tracking System* (ACTS) so that they could track both an individual child and the whole class progress. Using the *ACTS*, Bombeck teachers developed a method of organizing a wide range of data in a manageable system.

ACCESS calls upon teachers to use aggregated assessment data to make informed decisions about instruction.

The ACCESS Curriculum

The *ACCESS Curriculum* relies on an *Intentional Curriculum Decision-Making Cycle* (see figure 1-1) that:

1. Calls on early childhood professionals to evaluate the strengths, needs and resources to determine what is needed to provide high quality experiences for children;
2. Reflects the belief that young children learn best in intentionally planned environments that support active learning though play and other means throughout the day;
3. Implements high quality instruction that is dependent on strong teacher-child interactions in which teachers encourage inquiry, support play/active learning, and extend language and concept development; and
4. Uses aggregated and authentic assessment data to make instructional decisions and track child progress. These data are also used to inform program evaluation and continue the ongoing Intentional Curriculum Decision-Making Cycle.

Figure 1-1: Intentional Curriculum Decision-Making Cycle

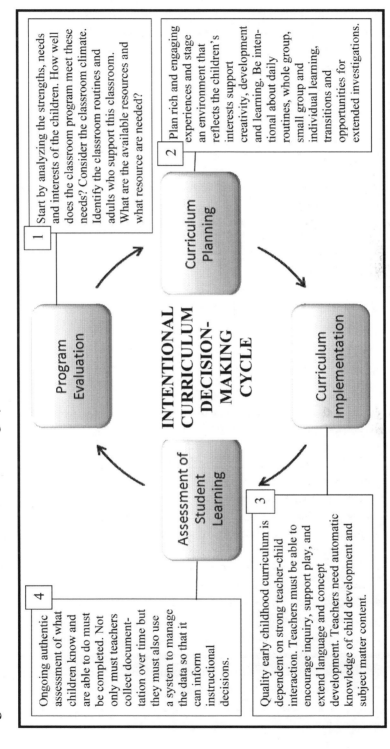

1 Start by analyzing the strengths, needs and interests of the children. How well does the classroom program meet these needs? Consider the classroom climate. Identify the classroom routines and adults who support this classroom. What are the available resources and what resource are needed?

2 Plan rich and engaging experiences and stage an environment that reflects the children's interests support creativity, development and learning. Be intentional about daily routines, whole group, small group and individual learning, transitions and opportunities for extended investigations.

3 Quality early childhood curriculum is dependent on strong teacher-child interaction. Teachers must be able to encourage inquiry, support play, and extend language and concept development. Teachers need automatic knowledge of child development and subject matter content.

4 Ongoing authentic assessment of what children know and are able to do must be completed. Not only must teachers collect documentation over time but they must also use a system to manage the data so that it can inform instructional decisions.

Curriculum Planning

Program Evaluation

INTENTIONAL CURRICULUM DECISION-MAKING CYCLE

Curriculum Implementation

Assessment of Student Learning

27

ACCESS asks early childhood educators to view the whole day as an opportunity for learning and assessment. Intentional planning enriches not only the investigations and mini-investigations that comprise a portion of the program but also the daily routines and "in-betweens" which refer to the transitions that occur while moving from one experience to another or from one investigation to another.

The ACCESS Curriculum Planning Process

The *ACCESS* Curriculum Planning Process utilizes the *Intentional Curriculum Decision-Making Cycle* that begins with the **evaluation** (see figure 1-1) of the strengths and needs of the program including:

- school culture, resources, limitations;
- curriculum focus from past years and the likely future focus;
- opportunities to facilitate the development of classroom community;
- daily routines that meet the needs of children and families and provide opportunities for meaningful and connected learning;
- opportunities for inquiry;
- ability to follow the children's interest;
- quality of the environment, materials and teacher-child interactions;
- accuracy and complexity of science concepts;
- an analysis of the children's aggregated assessment data; and
- reflects the children's family culture.

Then teaching teams collaboratively **plan** (See figure 1-1) high quality experiences including *investigations* and *mini-investigations* that support meaningful inquiry. Also intentionally planned are the *daily routines* and *in-betweens* that provide opportunities for children to develop and practice developmental skills and academic skills in meaningful and connected ways.

Teaching teams **implement** (See figure 1-1) the daily routines, in-betweens, investigations and mini-investigations keeping in mind that investigations and mini investigations comprise only part of the day or week. Daily routines and in-betweens encompass much of the children's time.

Next teachers **assess** (See figure 1-1) the children's development, interests and content knowledge through the observation of daily routines and play-based, small group, and large group experiences. Data are aggregated for the class as a whole across all subject areas and developmental domains and are used to make planning decisions. These data are also used to revisit program evaluation to continuously improve practice in order to meet the needs of children and families.

Investigations Investigations (See figure 1-2) constitute part of the day or week and connect learning around an important science topic for several weeks or months. Similar to the projects described in Katz and Chard's *Project Approach*, (2000), investigations are inquiry-based extended studies that require children to make observations and collect data in order to answer research questions.

- *Projects*, as described by Katz and Chard (2000), focus on topics worthy of study from a wide variety of disciplines.
- *Investigations* as described in *ACCESS,* focus on inquiry-based questions typically related to important science topics. Additionally, *ACCESS* includes an intentional system to track subject matter content and developmental skills.

Mini-Investigations Like the longer and more extensive "investigations," "mini-investigations" (See figure 1-2) also constitute only part of the day. The duration of the mini-investigation is shorter than a full investigation, generally lasting a week or two. This shorter duration allows teachers and children to focus time on less substantial studies of topics that are meaningful to children and families but may not be worthy of the time commitment associated with a full investigation. Common topics for mini-investigations include seasonal studies such as Thanksgiving or Earth Day. Mini-investigations also support the family cultures of programs that celebrate Cinco De Mayo or Chinese New Year. Other programs have long standing traditions that would be appropriate for a mini investigation. One preschool program in a public school setting joined the rest of the school in a weeklong celebration of Dr. Seuss' birthday. In another example, one class at the Bombeck Center conducted a two week mini-investigation on castles after the children expressed intense interest in the topic during a more extensive investigation on construction. Using Katz's strategies for choosing topics worthy of study, the teachers realized that children living in Ohio would have little if any experience with castles and the opportunities for inquiry were limited. The teachers also noted the intense interest that the children had in castle-like structures. During walks around campus, children noted the castle-like turrets on many of campus buildings and the entrance to nearby historic Woodland Cemetery. The children's interest continued each day on the playground as the children could see castle-like, Holy Angels Church from their playground. The "Mini Investigation" instructional category allowed the teachers to honor the children's interest by supporting a 2 week exploration of castles.

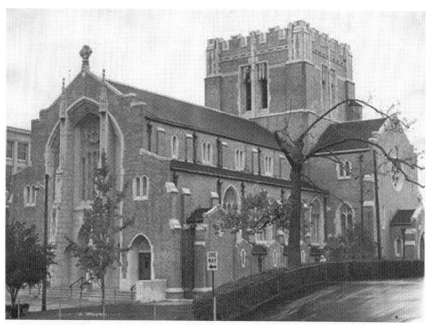

The view of Holy Angels Church from the Bombeck Center playground inspired an interest in castle-like structures during the Construction Investigation.

The entrance to nearby Woodland Cemetery.

St. Joesph's Hall at the University of Dayton.

Mini investigations allow teachers and children to incorporate the interests of children, teachers as well as, family and school culture in ways that are meaningful but do not warrant an extended investigation.

In-betweens In-betweens (See figure 1-2) refers to the times of transition between investigations. *ACCESS* emphasizes the importance of intentional planning and the need to capitalize on the learning opportunities that occur during transitions from one investigation to the next. *ACCESS* embraces the time "in-between" investigations as opportunities to discover children's interest, reflect on what children have learned by analyzing documentation and to build anticipation and excitement for the next investigation.

Daily Routines Daily routines (See figure 1-2) are the common structures of the day that provide young children with the comforting predictability that is part of a quality early childhood program. Whether taking part in snack time, engaging in a morning meeting, or putting on their coats to go outside, children can benefit from well planned routines that support development and learning. For older children, daily routines also include curriculum addressed regularly as part of the adopted reading and/or math program.

When intentionally planned, snack time for these infants provides opportunities for development across all domains.

Figure 1-2 *ACCESS*: Pulling It all Together Diagram

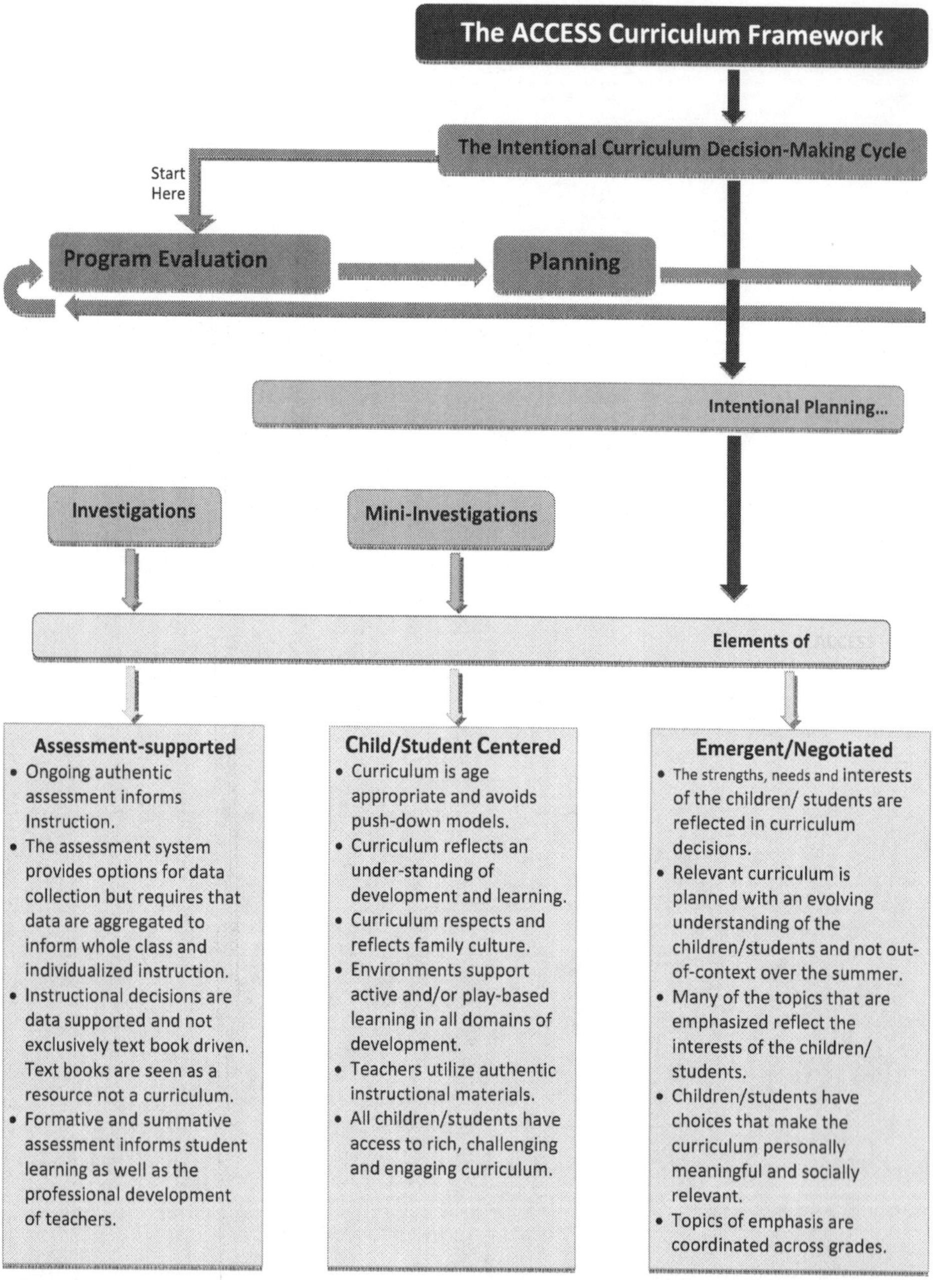

The ACCESS Curriculum Framework

The Intentional Curriculum Decision-Making Cycle

Start Here

Program Evaluation → Planning

Intentional Planning...

Investigations   Mini-Investigations

Elements of

Assessment-supported
- Ongoing authentic assessment informs Instruction.
- The assessment system provides options for data collection but requires that data are aggregated to inform whole class and individualized instruction.
- Instructional decisions are data supported and not exclusively text book driven. Text books are seen as a resource not a curriculum.
- Formative and summative assessment informs student learning as well as the professional development of teachers.

Child/Student Centered
- Curriculum is age appropriate and avoids push-down models.
- Curriculum reflects an under-standing of development and learning.
- Curriculum respects and reflects family culture.
- Environments support active and/or play-based learning in all domains of development.
- Teachers utilize authentic instructional materials.
- All children/students have access to rich, challenging and engaging curriculum.

Emergent/Negotiated
- The strengths, needs and interests of the children/ students are reflected in curriculum decisions.
- Relevant curriculum is planned with an evolving understanding of the children/students and not out-of-context over the summer.
- Many of the topics that are emphasized reflect the interests of the children/ students.
- Children/students have choices that make the curriculum personally meaningful and socially relevant.
- Topics of emphasis are coordinated across grades.

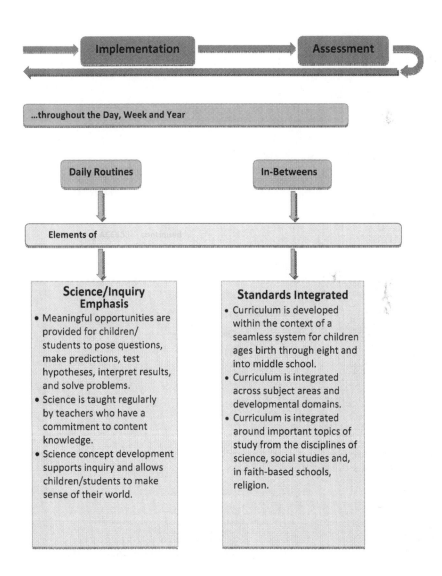

Implementation → Assessment

...throughout the Day, Week and Year

Daily Routines   In-Betweens

Elements of

Science/Inquiry Emphasis

- Meaningful opportunities are provided for children/students to pose questions, make predictions, test hypotheses, interpret results, and solve problems.
- Science is taught regularly by teachers who have a commitment to content knowledge.
- Science concept development supports inquiry and allows children/students to make sense of their world.

Standards Integrated

- Curriculum is developed within the context of a seamless system for children ages birth through eight and into middle school.
- Curriculum is integrated across subject areas and developmental domains.
- Curriculum is integrated around important topics of study from the disciplines of science, social studies and, in faith-based schools, religion.

The ACCESS Acronym

ACCESS is an acronym that represents the philosophical basis for the curriculum:

A *A*ssessment-supported
C *C*hild-
C *C*entered
E *E*mergent/Negotiated
S *S*cience emphasis
S *S*tandards integrated

Assessment-supported According to the National Association for the Education of Young Children (NAEYC) and the National Association of Early Childhood Specialists in State Departments of Education (NAECS/SDE) (2005), assessment is to be an integral component of the curriculum, with results used to guide teaching, identify concerns for individual children, and provide information to improve and guide interventions. Assessment methods to be used are those that are "developmentally appropriate, culturally and linguistically responsive, tied to children's daily activities, supported by professional development, and inclusive of families" (p. 2). In contrast to "assessment driven" which may invoke notions of "teaching to the test," ACCESS is "assessment supported" which refers to the system of ongoing documentation and recordkeeping that is done by teachers as they collect data on individual children and on the class as a whole. The *ACCESS* assessment system was designed by teachers and allows them to record information about the children's development and learning and also track where children are in terms of subject matter standards and developmental skills. Because the assessment system is such an integral part of *ACCESS*, data is aggregated using the *ACCESS Classroom Tracking System*(ACTS) and used to inform the decisions that teachers make as they plan instruction, including future investigations, mini-investigations, in-betweens and daily routines. Through *ACCESS*, early childhood professionals are equipped with the information necessary to make teaching intentional and play purposeful.

Child Centered Research shows that there are wide cultural variations in the experiences and developmental rates of young children, as well as in children's individual needs, including those of children with disabilities (Garcia-Coll & Magnuson, 2000; Sandall, McLean & Smith, 2000; Odom & Diamond, 1998). "Early learning standards should be flexible enough to encourage teachers and other professionals to embed culturally and individually relevant experiences in the curriculum, creating adaptations that promote success for all children" (NAEYC & NAECS/SDE, 2005, p. 6). *ACCESS* includes in its instructional decision-making process an emphasis on following the child's lead, allowing for child choice, providing ample opportunities for high levels of teacher-child interactions, and staging an environment that allows children to practice their evolving skills and explore their world through play.

Another strength of *ACCESS* is the emphasis on social and emotional development. Research has shown that early social and emotional competence predicts school readiness and later success (Ewing Marion Kaufmann Foundation, 2002; NAEYC & NAECS/SDE, 2002; Peth-Pierce, 2001; Raver, 2002, Cooper, Masi, & Vick, 2009, National Scientific Council on the Developing Child, 2007). Social and emotional development is supported by providing teachers and families with the skills needed to guide the typical behavior of young children and provide positive behavior supports, behavior analysis, and behavior management planning for children whose behavior is challenging and/or exceptional.

Emergent *ACCESS* relies, in part, on an emergent but negotiated curriculum model. Teachers plan instruction, select materials and stage environments that support investigations that emerge from the children's interests, realizing that children are motivated to learn concepts more thoroughly and permanently when they are meaningful, connected to prior knowledge, have a purpose, and apply to real life situations (Bredekamp & Copple, 1997; Copple & Bredekamp, 2009; NAEYC & NAECS/SDE, 2002). Based on *The Project Approach* (Helm & Katz, 2002; Katz & Chard, 2000), investigations emerge from the children's interests while also being funneled through the teachers' understanding of the children's developmental strengths and needs, an aggregated assessment of the children's content knowledge, a comprehensive view of content standards and developmental guidelines, an understanding of family culture and the richness of the questions generated by the children. The teacher is the informed evaluator who considers all of these variables to determine which topic is most worthy of an extended investigation.

One of the many benefits of a curriculum that is emergent and based on the study of important topics, is that children tend to be highly engaged in learning. The teacher assists children in the integration of concepts through group and individual discussions/experiences and supports children's attempts to explain their discoveries and construct their own theories. Children are provided with many materials which they will use to represent their understanding of the topic. Consistent with *The Project Approach* (Katz & Chard, 2000), children conduct field studies both inside and outside the classroom, rely on local experts to support their investigations and often culminate their work with an event that allows them to demonstrate their understanding of the topic and share their findings with others.

Based on the research supported by "Principles of Learning and Teaching" (Bedecamp & Copple, 1997; Copple & Bredecamp, 2009) investigations comprise only a portion of the children's day. Other activities and environments, both indoors and out-of-doors, are created to ensure that children have ample opportunity to develop and learn using a wide variety of developmentally appropriate materials and instructional strategies including small group activities such as learning centers, whole group activities including circle time or morning meetings, child directed activities such as dramatic and constructive play and indoor and outdoor "playscapes." The instruction that occurs throughout the day supports and inspires children to use existing skills and to develop new ones. It is important for children to have rich environments with ample authentic materials that appeal to a variety of ability levels. Many materials are selected because they can be used in both simplistic and complex ways meeting the needs of a wide variety of learners.

The young girl in this picture is captivated by a tree trunk that has been sliced into a life size 3 dimensional puzzle. She can choose to reconstruct the tree or explore the slices in unique and related ways.

Science Emphasis "From birth onward, humans, in their healthiest states, are active, inquisitive, curious, and playful creatures, displaying a ubiquitous readiness to learn and explore, and they do not require extraneous incentives to do so" (Ryan & Deci, 2000, p. 56). *ACCESS* capitalizes on these natural human tendencies and the intense sense of wonder that is present in young children and provides a curriculum that includes many opportunities for children to learn about science. Studying science topics allows teachers to build on children's natural curiosity by fostering a sense of wonder and by giving them the skills and tools they need to investigate their world. Science instruction also provides an engaging context through which students become literate, develop numeracy skills and academic language while they become more skilled socially. Because of the strong empirical evidence that shows that science instruction is not given adequate time in many early childhood programs and classrooms (Raizen & Michelsohn, 1994; Dorph, Shields, Tiffany-Morales, Hartry & McCaffrey, 2011), *ACCESS* provides a framework which supports science instruction and helps teachers find the time to teach this important subject area.

Quality curriculum for young children brings children and teachers together in rich interaction while both become captivated in learning about the world around them.

Standards Integrated One aspect of quality early childhood programming that is receiving national attention is the increasing emphasis on content knowledge for young children (Adams, Baldwin, Comingore, & Smith, 2006; Baldwin, Adams, & Kelly, 2009; Bredecamp & Pikulski, 2005, NAEYC & NAECS/SDE, 2002). Academic content standards are relatively new to early childhood and for many traditional early childhood educators, the notion of content appears to contradict the child-centered practice and emergent curriculum model that has been the philosophical foundation of most early childhood teacher preparation programs (Eliason & Jenkins, 2011; File & Kontos, 1993; Hyson, 2003). Some early childhood teachers struggle with the notion of how to blend an instructional focus on academic content with the NAEYC principles of learning and teaching that have been identified as preferred practice for the field of early childhood (Copple & Bredecamp 2009; Sandall, McLean, & Smith, 2000). At a time when there is a significant paradigm shift from a *purely* constructivist and play-based approach to preschool education, some early childhood professionals are surprised to learn that, under the right conditions, early learning content standards can create significant benefits for children's education and development while still maintaining a commitment to familiar developmentally appropriate practices (NAEYC & NAECS/SDE, 2002, 2005).

According to NAEYC and NAECS/SDE (2002 p. 4), "young children's development is strongly interconnected, with positive outcomes in one area relying on development in other domains." While many of the standards adopted by the states focus on the four academic content areas, *ACCESS* starts with a topic that is worthy of study, typically science, that includes both academic content standards and the developmental domains then integrate all three into the planning and assessment system. Teachers begin the planning process by watching children to determine a topic of study that has sparked the children's interest. Science topics are frequently chosen because children are "competent little scientists driven to move, to experiment, to know, and to connect with and learn from the people and the world around them" (Greenman, 2007, p 66). The topics of investigation provide a structure for the developmental domains and content areas to be integrated around a common theme that is socially relevant and meaningful to the children.

The toddlers in this picture are integrating new vocabulary as they use the language of motion while also developing social and large motor skills.

A Research-based Curriculum

The *ACCESS* Curriculum was developed to assist early childhood teachers to be intentional in their curriculum decision-making, is based on sound research, and has been field-tested at the Bombeck Center and in other early childhood classrooms. Efforts to insure that the curriculum is a valid, reliable, evidence-based tool that results in engaging and effective classroom environments, strong teacher-child interactions and deep concept development are described in the following sections.

Content Validity *ACCESS* is based on extensive research that identifies young children as active learners who draw on direct physical and social experience as well as culturally transmitted knowledge to construct their understandings of the world around them (Beaty, 2007; Bredecamp & Copple,

1997; Copple & Bredecamp, 2009; Epstein, Schweinhart, & McAdoo, 1996; File & Kontos, 1993; Howes & Smith, 1995; NAEYC & NAECS/SDE 2002, 2005; National Research Council, 2000; Peisner-Feinberg et al., 2001; Peth-Pierce, 2001; Raver, 2002; Sandall, McLean, & Smith, 2000; Wortham, 2010). Additionally, *ACCESS* incorporates the findings of the National Math Panel (2008), the National Early Literacy Panel (2008), and studies conducted by the National Institute for Early Education Research (NIEER); the National Scientific Council on the Developing Child, the PEW Center on the States and other key research studies that inform how best to meet the needs of young children in the 21st Century (Early, Maxwell, Burchinal, Alva, Bender, Bryant, et al., 2007).

Aligned with Professional Association Standards In addition to the professional organizations that represent the academic content standards of English/language arts, math, science, and social studies found in nationally recognized content standards, *ACCESS* also incorporates recommendations for preferred practice as defined by both the National Association for the Education of Young Children (NAEYC) and the Division of Early Childhood for the Council of Exceptional Children (DEC). The NAEYC and DEC recommendations work together to establish ideals that are blended in order to demonstrate preferred practice for children who are typically developing and those with special learning needs. *ACCESS* also reflects the 2002 joint position statement on early learning content standards developed by NAEYC and the National Association of Early Childhood Specialists in State Departments of Education (NAECS/SDE) (2005) which supports the inclusion of early learning content and emphasizes the principals of learning and teaching that comprise developmentally appropriate practice.

Construct Validity The construct validity of *ACCESS* was assessed in part through the use of *Head Start's Alignment Review Tool* (National Center on Quality Teaching and Learning, 2011) (see findings in Appendix A) which was used to verify that *ACCESS* aligns with the domains and domain elements identified in the *Head Start Child Development and Early Learning Framework* (Head Start Resource Center, 2010). Additionally, *ACCESS* has been successfully aligned with the *Common Core State Standards* (Association of American Governors and the Council of State Chief Education Officers, 2009), *Ohio's Learning and Development Standards* (Ohio Department of Education, 2013) and the *Ohio Infant and Toddler Guidelines* (Ohio Child Care Resource and Referral Association, 2006). While *ACCESS* was developed, field tested and implemented using the Ohio standards and guidelines, the developers found that it can be used with any developmentally appropriate set of curriculum standards, scope and sequence, or graded course of study and developmental skills across all domains.

Field-tested The components of *ACCESS* have been developed and practiced by teachers at the Bombeck Center who were observed and evaluated regularly to ensure the curriculum was being implemented consistently. Each teaching team met monthly with the curriculum specialist to reflect on practice, provide feedback and to ensure that curriculum planning decisions were made using the *ACCESS Intentional Curriculum Decision-Making Process*, the *Science Concept Planner* and the *ACCESS Classroom Tracking Sheet* (ACTS). Teams also discussed how daily routines and transitions were being used as important opportunities for learning. Follow-up was completed with both informal observations conducted by the curriculum specialist, center director and early childhood faculty. Formal assessment was conducted by external reviewers using the *Classroom Assessment Scoring System*(CLASS) (Pianta, LaParo, Hamre, 2008), *Early Childhood Environment Rating Scale-Revised* (ECERS) (Harms, Clifford & Cryer, 2004), and the *Infant Toddler Environment Rating Scale-Revised* (ITERS) (Harms, Cryer, & Clifford, 2006).

Once sufficient evidence was gathered to confirm that *ACCESS* was being consistently implemented across all classrooms at the Bombeck Center, field testing expanded to partners who were using components of *ACCESS* with preschoolers and children in kindergarten and the primary grades in child care, Head Start, private/Catholic and public school settings. Outside of the Bombeck Center, *ACCESS* was field tested using standardized training with pre and post training surveys and follow-up site visits which included classroom-based structured observations, interviews and pre/post assessment using valid and reliable standardized tools such as the CLASS (Pianta, LaParo, Hamre, 2008), ECERS-r (Harms, Clifford & Cryer, 2004), ITERS-r (Harms, Cryer, & Clifford, 2006), and the less formal *Science Environment Rating Scale* (Kelly, Adams, Baldwin & Comingore, 2009). Field testing was conducted in classrooms that serve children birth through age 8 across multiple socio-economic levels including those in poverty as well as with typically developing and at-risk children and those with special learning needs.

Results of Field Testing The results of field testing show *ACCESS* to be a practical, affordable and effective educational approach for young children across the early care and education continuum. For more information on how *ACCESS* was field tested see http:/accesscurriculum.com.

Summary

The *ACCESS Curriculum* is based on the belief that children are unique, capable individuals who are able to construct their own knowledge. It is grounded in early childhood research and theory, and knowledge of early childhood development. *ACCESS* is framed by the seven significant areas of development: social, emotional, language, cognitive, physical and health, motor, aesthetic and approaches to learning including executive functioning. The curriculum affords children the opportunity to grow in their understanding of their worlds through extended investigations. Topics for investigation are determined through observation of the children's interests while suitability of the topic for study is based on the topics relevance to the children, the opportunity for direct investigation, readily available resources, ease of representation through a variety of media and ability to support children's development and learning of age appropriate content. This *emergent* form of curriculum allows children, through structured and unstructured play/active learning, to process and reflect upon their experiences as they develop in a community of learners. Through the use of *ACCESS*, learning is supported by ongoing program evaluation and individual assessment. Aggregated authentic assessment provides for an in-depth understanding of the children and their learning enabling *ACCESS* to be a living document, a curriculum used to meet both individual and group needs.

References

Baldwin, J. L., Adams, S. M., & Kelly, M. K. (2009). Science at the center: An emergent, standards-based, child-centered framework for early learners. *Early Childhood Education Journal, 37*(2), 71-77.

Beaty, J. (2007). *Skills for preschool teachers* (8th ed.). Columbus, OH: Pearson-Merrill/Prentice Hall.

Bowman, B. T. (2006). Standards at the heart of educational equity. *Young Children, 61*(9): 42-48.

Bredecamp, S., & Pikulski, J. J. (2005). *Principles of an effective preschool curriculum.* Presentation at the National Association for the Education of Young Children conference, Washington, DC.

Bredecamp, S., & Copple, C. (1997). *Developmentally appropriate practice in early childhood programs: Birth to age 8* (2nd ed.). Washington DC: National Association for the Education of Young Children.

Cooper, J. L., Masi, R., & Vick, J. (2009). *Social-emotional development in early childhood: What every policymaker should know.* New York: National Center for Children in Poverty.

Copple, C., & Bredecamp, S. (Eds.). (2009). *Developmentally appropriate practice in early childhood programs: Serving children from birth to age 8* (3rd ed.). Washington DC: National Association for the Education of Young Children.

Dorph, R., Shields, P., Tiffany-Morales, J., Hartry, A., McCaffrey, T. (2011). *High hopes—few opportunities: The status of elementary science education in California.* Sacramento, CA: The Center for the Future of Teaching and Learning at West Ed.

Early, D. M., Maxwell, K. L., Burchinal, M., Alva, S., Bender, R., Bryant, D., et al. (2007). Teachers' education, classroom quality, and young children's academic skills: Results from seven studies of preschool programs. *Child Development, 78,* 558-580.

Eliason, C., & Jenkins, L. (2011). *A practical guide to early childhood curriculum* (6th ed.). Columbus, OH: Merrill/Prentice Hall.

Elkind, D. (1987). *Miseducation: Preschoolers at risk.* New York: Knopf.

Epstein, A. S., Schweinhart, L. J., & McAdoo, L. (1996). *Models of early childhood education.* Ypsilanti, MI: High/Scope Press.

Ewing Marion Kaufmann Foundation (2002). Set for success: Building a strong foundation for school readiness based on social-emotional development of young children. *Kaufman Early Education Exchange, 1*(1), 1-100.

File, N. K., & Kontos, S. (1993). The relationship of program quality to children's play in integrated early intervention settings. *Topics in Early Childhood Special Education,* 13, 1-18.

Frede E., & Ackerman, D. J., (2007). Preschool curriculum decision-making: Dimensions to consider. *Preschool Policy Brief.* 12. Brunswick, NJ: National Institute for Early Education Research.

Garcia-Coll, C., & Magnuson, K. (2000). Cultural differences as sources of developmental vulnerabilities and resources. In J. P. Shonkoff & S. J. Meisels (Eds.), *Handbook of Early Intervention* (pp. 94-114). New York: Cambridge University Press.

Greenman, J. (2007, March/April). The child's job: Talking to parents about child development. *Exchange,* 66-70.

Harms, T., Clifford, R. M., & Cryer, D. (2004). *Early childhood environment rating scale-revised.* New York: Teachers College Press.

Harms, T., Cryer, D., & Clifford, R. M. (2006). *Infant toddler environment rating scale-revised.* New York: Teachers College Press.

Head Start Resource Center (2010). *The Head Start child development and early learning framework promoting positive outcomes in early childhood programs serving children 3-5 years old.* Arlington, VA: Office of Head Start, Administration for Children and Families, U.S. Department of Health and Human Services.

Helm, J., & Katz, L. G. (2002). *Young investigators: The project approach in the early years.* New York: Teachers College Press.

Howes, C., & Smith, E. W. (1995). Relations among child care quality, teacher behavior, children's play activities, emotional security, and cognitive activity in child care. *Early Childhood Research Quarterly,* 10(4), 381-404.

Hyson, M. (2003). *Preparing early childhood professionals: NAEYC's standards for programs.* Washington, DC: National Association for the Education of Young Children.

Katz, L. G., & Chard, S. C. (2000). *Engaging children's minds: The project approach* (2nd ed.). Norwood, NJ: Ablex.

Maxwell, K. L., & Clifford, R. M. 2004. Research in review: School readiness assessment. *Young Children, 59*(1): 42-46.

Nagy, W., & Townsend, D. (2011). Words as tools: Learning academic vocabulary as language acquisition. *Reading Research Quarterly, 47* (1): 91-108.

National Association for the Education of Young Children. (2005). *NAEYC code of ethical conduct and statement of commitment.* Washington DC: author.

National Association for the Education of Young Children and the National Association of Early Childhood Specialists in State Departments of Education. (2002). *Early learning standards: Creating the conditions for success.* Joint Position /statement. Online: www.naeyc.org/dap.

National Association for the Education of Young Children and the National Association of Early Childhood Specialists in State Departments of Education. (2005). *Joint position statement on early childhood curriculum, assessment, and program evaluation.* Washington, DC: Authors.

National Center on Quality Teaching and Learning. (2011). *Curriculum, assessment and the Head Start framework: An alignment review tool.* Retrieved from (http://eclkc.ohs.acf.hhs.gov/hslc/tta-system/teaching/docs/Alignment-Guide-2.pdf).

National Governors Association Center for Best Practices and the Council of Chief State School Officers. (2011).*Common core state standards initiative.* Washington DC: author.

National Research Council. (2011). *A framework for k-12 science education: Practices, crosscutting concepts, and core ideas.* Committee on a Conceptual Framework for New K-12 Science Education Standards. Board on Science Education, Division of Behavioral and Social Sciences and Education. Washington, DC: The National Academies Press.

National Research Council and Institute of Medicine. (2000). *From neurons to neighborhoods: The science of early childhood development.* Committee on Integrating the Science of Early Childhood Development, Shonkoff J.,

Phillips D. (eds.). Board on Children, Youth, and Families, Commission on Behavioral and Social Sciences and Education. Washington, DC, National Academy Press.

National Scientific Council on the Developing Child. (2007). *The science of early childhood development.* Cambridge, MA: Harvard University. (Retrieved 11/16/2011) http://www.developingchild.net.

New, R. (1999). Playing fair and square: Issues of equity in preschool mathematics, science and technology. In American Association for the Advancement of Science, *Dialogue on early childhood science, mathematics and technology education.* Washington, DC: author.

Odom, S. L., & Diamond K. E. (Eds.). 1998. Inclusion of young children with special needs in early childhood education: The research base. *Early Childhood Research Quarterly, 13*(1), 3-25.

Ohio Department of Education. (2010). *Ohio early learning content standards.* Columbus, Oh: author.

Ohio Child Care Resource and Referral Association, (2006). *Ohio infant and toddler guidelines* Columbus, Ohio: Author.

Peisner-Feinberg, E. S., Burchinal, M. R., Clifford, R. M., Culkin, M. L., Howes, C., Kagan, S. L., et al. (2001). *The relation of preschool child-care quality to children's cognitive and social developmental trajectories through second grade. Child Development, 72*(5), 1534-1553.

Peth-Pierce, R. (2001). *A good beginning: Sending America's children to school with the social emotional competence they need to succeed.* Child Mental Health Foundations and Agencies Network (FAN) Monograph. Bethesda, MD: National Institute of Mental Health, Office of Communications and Public Liaison.

Pianta, R. C., LaParo, K. M., & Hamre, B. K. (2007). *Classroom Assessment Scoring System.* Baltimore, MD: Brookes Publishing.

Raizen, S. A. and Michelsohn, A. M. (1994). *The future of science in elementary schools.* San Fransico: Jossey-Bass

Raver, C. C. (2002). *Emotions matter: Making the case for the role of young children's emotional development for early school readiness.* Ann Arbor, MI: Society for Research in Child Development.

Ryan, R. M., & Deci, E. L. (2000). Intrinsic and extrinsic motivations: Classic definitions and new directions. *Contemporary Educational Psychology, 25,* 54-67.

Sandall, S., McLean, M., & Smith, B. (2000). *DEC recommended practices in early intervention/early childhood special education.* Longmont, CO: Sopris West.

Wortham, S. C. (2010). *Early childhood curriculum: Developmental bases for learning and teaching* (5th ed.). Upper Saddle River, NJ: Prentice Hall.

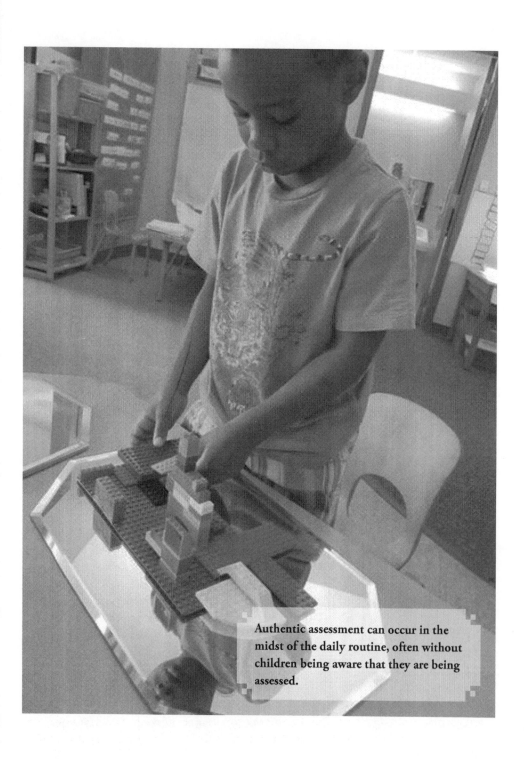

Authentic assessment can occur in the midst of the daily routine, often without children being aware that they are being assessed.

2

Assessment-Supported

When materials and procedures accommodate a child's sensory, response, affective, and cultural characteristics, they are equitable. (DEC Recommended Practices: Assessment, 2005, p.49).

Many types of standardized tests are available for use with infants and young children. All are psychological tests, whether they measure abilities, achievements, aptitudes, interests, attitudes, values, or personality characteristics (Wortham, 2012, p. 53).

Early childhood intervention requires assessment procedures that are designed and field validated specifically for young children with disabilities, capture real-life competencies in everyday routines, help plan individual programs, and document incremental improvements in developmental competencies. Conventional tests and testing, which have dominated measurement in the field, fail to meet early intervention purposes and published professional recommended practice standards (Bagnato, 2005, p. 17).

Instruction that is assessment-supported refers to the practice of using authentic and naturally occurring assessment data to inform instructional decisions. In contrast, instruction that is assessment-driven focuses more on student progress and program quality data which are often misused to make instructional decisions. Assessment-driven instruction often has improved progress scores as its goal and the end result is a scenario in which curriculum becomes a series of unrelated concepts and activities that are presented out of context and that cover material at a surface level. Effective assessment for young children is very different from that of older children. Where older children can read and write, preschoolers, toddlers and infants show what they know and are able to do through different means. This difference requires that early childhood educators be extremely capable observers of children (Beaty, 2005). They must be able to document what they see children do and must be able to present that documentation in a manner that is meaningful to parents, candidates, other teachers and to the children themselves. Assessment-supported curriculum refers to an ongoing cycle of assessment to instruction to assessment. While we believe in the importance of multiple means of assessment, including assessment for student progress and assessment for program improvement, we are very careful to use data only for those purposes for which it was intended and for which the results are valid and reliable. We believe in the collaborative nature of assessment and data collection (Linder, 2008), and support candidates to be members of transdisciplinary teams who collect assessment data, interpret it, and organize and present it in the form of classroom documentation boards, student portfolios and anecdotal records. The data that we collect supports our understanding of what children know and are able to do and becomes an important consideration in the selection of investigation topics, materials, environments and experiences.

Why Assess?

- *Why do we need an assessment system?*
- *We know the children are learning. Young children continuously learn and display new skills.*
- *You want me to sit at a table and ask the child to cut and color on demand?*

Sound familiar? Assessment could be the four-letter word of early childhood education! There may be some very good reasons for this aversion as assessment for young children has historically been inappropriate. Often assessment practices have included methods that were designed for older children or were designed to evaluate programs for older children. Assessors who did not understand child development and program evaluators who did not understand quality indicators for early childhood programs have left many in the field skeptical of the whole assessment process.

Assessment is now a part of early care and education programs, as are early learning content standards developed by state departments of education

(Baldwin, Adams, & Kelly, 2009; National Association for the Education of Young Children and the National Association of Early Childhood Specialists in State Departments of Education, 2003). State and federally funded child care and education programs are mandated to document that children are progressing through and meeting or exceeding the early learning content standards. Even those programs that are not impacted by state and federal mandates are challenged to ensure that the children they serve have access to the state adopted academic content. The premise is that standardizing the academic content that young children should know and be able to do before entering kindergarten will "level the playing field" for children who are at risk for school failure. Before the development of academic content standards, there was no common definition of kindergarten readiness. Even those who served children who were not considered to be at risk, struggled to prepare children to be "ready" when the definition differed from teacher to teacher, school to school, and district to district.

Assessment of Development

Teachers in the field of early care and education have traditionally monitored the development of the children in their care. They know typical child development and are aware if a child is not following that expected pattern (Beaty, 2005). The use of formal, standardized testing was not part of the typical developmental assessment system, unless a child was suspected of or identified as having a disability (Meisels & Atkins-Burnett, 2000). But, even at that point, the word "assessment" still conjures up the picture of the school psychologist sitting the child at a table and "testing" him/her in unfamiliar surroundings, with out-of-context materials, and without the benefit of having a parent or care-giver nearby (Bagnato, Neisworth & Munson, 1997; Linder, 2008).

Developmental skills present themselves throughout the day. Naturally occurring events like this one provides an example of how developmental domains overlap. An observer of this scene could easily document both physical and social skills.

In an effort to improve the results of assessment of young children, Neisworth and Bagnato (2004) support an authentic assessment model that utilizes the child's natural environment and daily activities to provide the information required to make decisions about young children's developmental levels and/or programmatic needs. They have developed eight assessment-related standards which are tied to the professional practice standards adopted by the Division for Early Childhood (DEC) of the Council for Exceptional Children (CEC). Six of the eight standards directly refer to instruments, formal and informal, used in preschool settings. The standards related to instruments delineate the usefulness of the instrument, the acceptability of the tool by professionals and families, the use of natural methods and context, and the adaptability for children with special needs. In addition, the assessment-related standards suggest that all ecological data be considered in the interpretation of the results and that there is professional/ parent collaboration.

Assessment in kindergarten through grade 3 also has become more "high stakes" with state and national testing required in the third grade to assess content knowledge in reading and mathematics. What used to be weekly spelling tests and assessment of math facts has now turned into "testing" and related test preparation. Informal assessments to inform instruction have morphed into teaching and testing of content standards, particularly in the area of reading. Using assessments to inform curricular decisions has dropped out of primary grades as the "curriculum" has become all about programmed reading and mathematics instruction. Science and social studies are seldom part of the daily classroom instructional time in today's schools.

Implications for Infants and Toddlers

Assessment across all age levels is important for tracking development and understanding what a child knows and shows teachers how to plan future classroom activities. For infants and toddlers, tracking development can help identify red flags for childhood disorders such as Autism as well as other developmental delays addressed across one or more domains. Using formative tools helps teachers to understand how infants and toddlers are developing and what teachers need to work on specifically to help develop individual skills and plan future learning activities.

Assessment Supported Curriculum

According to the National Association for the Education of Young Children (NAEYC) and the National Association for Early Childhood Specialists in State Departments of Education (NAECS/SDE), assessment is to be an integral component of the curriculum, with results used to guide teaching, identify concerns for individual children, and provide information to improve and guide interventions. Assessment methods to be used are those that are "developmentally appropriate, culturally and linguistically responsive, tied to children's daily activities, supported by professional development, and inclusive of families" (NAEYC/NAECS/SDE, 2003, p. 2).

Indicators of effective assessment systems include:

- Ethical principles guide assessment practices
- Assessment instruments are used for their intended purposes
- Assessments are appropriate for ages and other characteristics of children being assessed
- Assessment instruments are in compliance with professional criteria for quality
- What is assessed is developmentally and educationally significant
- Assessment evidence is used to understand and improve learning
- Assessment evidence is gathered from realistic settings and situations that reflect children's actual performance
- Assessments use multiple sources of evidence gathered over time
- Screening is always linked to follow-up
- Use of individually administered, norm-referenced tests is limited
- Staff and families are knowledgeable about assessment

(NAEYC, 2003)

How does this apply to child-care, preschool programs, and the primary grades? They too must be accountable, and be able to document that children are learning in their programs, particularly the state early learning content standards and K-3rd grade state and national standards. The challenge becomes to find a workable system that is teacher and child friendly, fits into the daily activities, and in the case of the University of Dayton's Bombeck Family Learning Center (Bombeck Center), values and works with an emergent curriculum model. As the curriculum and assessment development process evolved at the Bombeck Center, the first step was to figure out what the teachers would prefer to be included in the system. As staff discussed the more typical types of assessment tools for early childhood, they realized that the key to all types of assessment was strong observational skills.

Mindes (2007) states "the cornerstone of an assessment system is child observation" (p. 59). Teachers observe children on a continual basis, and use that information to make decisions about class content, individual child development, and possible need for more in-depth assessment if a child is not meeting developmental skills as expected. Regardless of the documentation system chosen, the key is to be a good observer of child behavior.

A skilled observer can document how this child handles a book, whether he "reads" from left to right, if he distinguishes picture from print, and numerous other content standards and developmental skills.

Implications for Infants and Toddlers

Using assessment to guide curriculum goals allows teachers the opportunity to know where children are developmentally and use the results to plan learning experiences around areas of need. Especially with infants and toddlers, it is important to individualize the curriculum and make sure that each child has the opportunity to work with teachers and other students to build on previous experiences that enhance development across all domains. Assessing infants and toddlers is more authentic when using an observational method because learning is not yet centered on academics but more on emotional growth and social interactions which occur every day in natural settings.

It is important to maintain authentic and natural assessments with very young children and at the Bombeck Family Learning Center, teachers use a variety of strategies to compile information on the development of infants and toddlers. Being a keen observer of children is key to this process and knowledge of child development helps teachers make the most out of their time observing children. Some of the assessment strategies used by Bombeck teachers include portfolio documentation including photos, Infant/Toddler Guidelines Checklists, and anecdotal notes, as well as samples of children's work.

Another form of assessment used by Bombeck staff includes the *Ages and Stages Questionnaire* (ASQ), which is a developmental checklist for infants and toddlers that covers all developmental domains including communication, gross motor, fine motor, problem solving (cognitive), and personal-social. These domains are imperative for observation because they are the foundation for all future learning as children grow and build on prior experiences.

Teachers at the Bombeck Center are able to track students' development throughout the first three years of life as they grow and learn. The ASQ and the portfolio pages cover many developmental domains and are able to be cross-referenced so that teachers have a variety of assessments that delineate where a child is developmentally. The use of portfolios is a well-documented means to support child-centered learning, and also allows teachers to reflect on their teaching, plan effectively, and involve families. Figure 2-1 is an example of a portfolio page that uses Ohio's Infant/Toddler Guidelines as a way to document student learning.

Figure 2-1: Infant and Toddler Portfolio Page

Language and Communication Development

Infant/Toddler Guidelines	Evidence:
□ **Understanding Language:** The child will comprehend the message of another's communication.	
□ **Expressing Language:** The child will convey a message or transfer information to another person.	
□ **Rules of Language:** The child will participate in interactions with language that follow the expected practices of the child's family and community.	
□ **Early Reading:** The child will demonstrate interest in book reading, storytelling and singing and will eventually understand the meaning of basic symbols.	
□ **Early Writing:** The child will demonstrate interest in writing and will develop the fine motor abilities required to hold a writing tool and make marks on a surface.	

Developing a Comprehensive System of Assessment

Where to Start—Evaluate Program Resources

Start by analyzing the strengths, needs and interests of the children. How well does the classroom program meet these needs? Identify the classroom routines and adults who support this classroom. What are the available resources and what resources are needed?

Identify Classroom Culture and Climate Every classroom has both a culture and a climate that determines who makes up the classroom and how the classroom functions. Classroom culture refers to both the history and traditions of the classroom, program and/or school as well as those of the teachers and children who are a part of the classroom. When identifying classroom culture, look at where the classroom is located. Is the classroom located in a public or private school, stand-alone location or as a part of a Head Start site? If the classroom has a team of teachers, discover how long the individual teachers have been teaching and also how long have they been together. The history and traditions of the classroom may need to defer to research based and developmentally appropriate practice, however, they are powerful forces that need to come to the surface and be part of the critical reflection process.

Where culture is influenced by the history of the classroom, climate refers to the present. Climate describes the day to day emotions that are part of the functioning of the classroom. Climate is the emotional tone of the classroom that can be represented by joyful learning, total chaos, or constricted actions and behaviors. Climate can be impacted by the age of children, gender make-up and interactions in the peer group. The teacher or teaching team is responsible for setting the tone that steers classroom climate and intentional planning and reflection is a vital step in creating a climate that is conducive to learning and development. We start by considering the following questions:

1. Who are the children and what is typical for their age?
2. What are the strengths, needs and interests of individual children?
3. What is the family culture, strengths, needs and interests?
4. What is the school culture and what are the school traditions that impact curriculum? Does the school have certain topics of study that are repeated at a specific age or grade level? Are there whole program

celebrations that are part of the school's tradition? Are their certain topics that are overused?

5. What resources are available and what are lacking?
6. What is the quality of the early childhood environment? Can I conduct an audit of the environment using such tools as the ITERS-R or ECERS-R (Harms, 2003)?
7. Are there mandated screenings or assessments required by the program? What data currently exist?

It is important that all members of the teaching team take part in establishing the classroom routines and philosophy. Start by identifying the different adults and their roles in the classroom. Identify any other support staff and their roles that influence both the children and classroom staff. Is there an intervention specialist or other therapists that provide direct services to the children or a curriculum director or site supervisor that provides direct support to the teaching staff? Is everyone aware of the grouping routines, daily schedule, rules, strategies for guiding behavior and other site specific information that aids in understanding classroom context? Have intentional conversations so that everyone in the teaching team is not only aware of the routines but also understands their purpose.

The ACCESS Assessment System

Before a good documentation system can be developed, the purpose of the system must be established. With the national movement to adopt content standards for young children, educators, including the teachers at the Bombeck Center, struggle with how to stay true to the developmentally appropriate curriculum principles that espouse the importance of play-based and emergent curriculum models. University faculty and Bombeck Center teachers have found that content standards can be taught within the context of a play-based and emergent curriculum framework if instructional decisions are supported by appropriate assessment (Baldwin, et al., 2009). An assessment supported curriculum system also provides a venue for teachers to come to a deeper and more connected understanding of state early learning standards, such as the Ohio Early Learning Content Standards (ELCS; Ohio Department of Education [DOE], 2004). At the Bombeck Center, a "divide and conquer" approach was used, with each teacher taking a set of indicators to review and cross-reference as other teachers discussed the indicators on their list. In this manner, it became apparent that there was repetition and overlap among the areas of mathematics, science, social studies and English language arts. Adjustments were made to the standards in order to reduce this redundancy and repetition. Through this process, the teachers became more aware of the standards to be observed and/or assessed in their classrooms.

During these discussions with the Center staff, three components of the ACCESS assessment system emerged. First, the teachers liked anecdotal record keeping and felt this was a good way to document child development and learning while maintaining accurate information for reporting to parents. Second, they liked the idea of portfolios for documenting both ELCS and development. Finally, they saw the importance of using checklists to assess everyday activities and discreet skills, as well as for documenting whole class involvement with the ELCS.

Anecdotal Records "are brief, accurate notes made of significant events or critical incidents in a particular child's day" (Mindes, 2007, p. 67). These should include identifying information about the child/children, provide a continuous description of the behavior observed, provide enough detail to document the child/children's behaviors, record what happens only during that observation period, and be interpreted at a later date (Gallagher, as cited in Henniger, 1999). The teachers at the Bombeck Center developed a few different strategies for documenting child progress and skills through the use of anecdotal records.

The most consistent method used with a variety of documentation sheets involving peel and stick labels located on clipboards stationed around the room in various center and/or play areas. Teachers made notes about what the children were doing as it was observed, and often tried to snap photos of the child in the activity to help with documentation of the standard or developmental skill (Annotated Photographs). These notes, and pictures if available, were later transferred to an investigation or standards documentation form (Figure 2-2). Additional information regarding the specifics of the sample was added, and the paper was placed in the child's portfolio, after the information was transferred to the whole class tracking system if appropriate.

Figure 2-2 Grace's Annotated Photograph with Checklist

Standards Covered:

___Explore and identify parts and wholes of familiar objects

X Explore and compare materials that provide many different sensory experiences

___Explore ways of moving objects in different ways

___Explore musical instruments and objects and manipulate one's own voice to recognize the changes in sound

X Identify the intended purpose of familiar tools

X Use familiar objects to accomplish a purpose, complete a task, or solve a problem

X Demonstrate the safe use of tools

___Ask questions about objects, organisms, pictures, letters, signs, and events

X Show interest in investigating unfamiliar objects, organisms, and phenomena during shared stories, conversations, and play

___Participate in simple, spontaneous scientific explorations with others

Science
Physical Science, Science and Technology, and Scientific Inquiry

This one holds the most water because it is bigger. - Grace S.

6-20-07

Teacher Reflection:

Grace is able to change the amount of water in the containers using the tools provided. She understands vocabulary related to size and comparison. She is ready to learn more about measuring and ordering.

Running records are considered a more detailed record of a child's behavior with the observer documenting everything that occurs within a short period of time. The teachers at the Bombeck Center felt running records provided good information but simply required too much time and attention from the teacher for just one child when there were several children in the room.

Checklists can be purchased, but often teachers develop their own. Four steps in creating a checklist, as offered by Wortham (2008), include identifying the skills to be included, listing the behaviors to be observed separately, sequencing the checklist in order of complexity or difficulty, and developing a simple method of record keeping. The lists then become "a framework for assessment and evaluation, instructional planning, record keeping, and communicating with parents about what is being taught and how their child is progressing" (Wortham, 2005, p. 120). The teachers at the Bombeck Center utilize checklists based on the Ohio Early Learning Content Standards (Ohio DOE, 2004). These are predominately a clumping of standards that can work easily together, with space for documenting individual child responses. For example, social studies standards around sharing, working together and cooperative behavior were combined for a checklist that can be used for monitoring behavior and activities either indoors or outside as children engage in play with their peers (see Figure 2-3). Within the primary grades, teachers rely on checklist for quick monitoring of a child's learning and/or understanding of the content.

Figure 2-3: Annotated Documentation—Social Studies 3

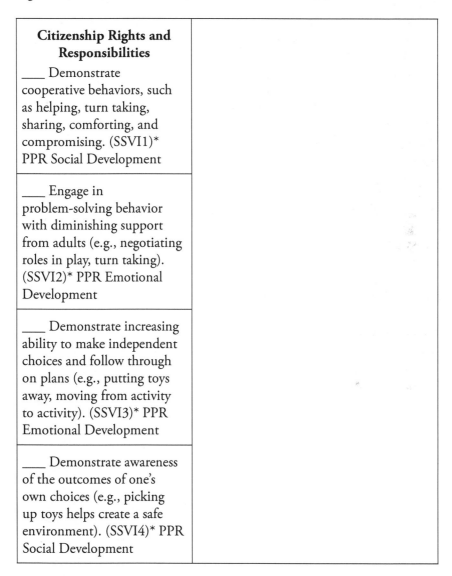

Citizenship Rights and Responsibilities	
____ Demonstrate cooperative behaviors, such as helping, turn taking, sharing, comforting, and compromising. (SSVI1)* PPR Social Development	
____ Engage in problem-solving behavior with diminishing support from adults (e.g., negotiating roles in play, turn taking). (SSVI2)* PPR Emotional Development	
____ Demonstrate increasing ability to make independent choices and follow through on plans (e.g., putting toys away, moving from activity to activity). (SSVI3)* PPR Emotional Development	
____ Demonstrate awareness of the outcomes of one's own choices (e.g., picking up toys helps create a safe environment). (SSVI4)* PPR Social Development	

Social Studies Skills and Methods ___ Gain information through participation in experiences with objects, media, books, and engaging in conversations with peers. (SSVII1)* ACTS ELA 10b, S9	
___ Begin to make predictions (e.g., guess whether other countries around the world celebrate birthdays). (SSVII2)* ACTS S9	
___ Represent ideas through multiple forms of language and expression (e.g., drawing, dramatic play, conversation, art media, music, movement, emergent writhing). (SSVII3)* ACTS ELA 3,10	

Teacher Reflection:

Observer:

* *Guidelines for ELCS Implementation*, ODE 2005, rev. 2006

Performance-based Assessments are often also called **authentic assessments** and measure what a child can do, as well as what they know, as one generally has to know a concept before being able to apply it. Within this curriculum framework, various types of performance assessments are utilized, predominately **interviews**, **work samples, investigations,** and **portfolios.** Teachers are frequently observed talking with children about what they are doing. This communication, based around questions asked by the teacher and more questions dependent on the child's response, allows the teacher to assess the child's knowledge and thinking process. This information may be documented on one of the Annotated Documentation forms, or included on a checklist designed specifically for the skills or concepts being assessed (see Figure 2-4: Worms Investigation Standards Documentation sheet).

Figure 2-4 WORMS Investigation Standards Documentation

WORMS Investigation Standards Documentation
March/April 2007

Standards	Child's Name: _____
_____ELF11 Demonstrate or orally communicate position and directional words (ELAII4), attributes (eg. Taller, heavier, more, etc.) (MII4), (M/SR/5), and motion related words (SIII4)	Date: _____ Documentation/Evidence:
_____ELCS16 Predict what might happen next during the reading of text. (ELAIII5)	
_____ELCS17 Connect information or ideas in text prior knowledge and experience (ELAIII6, ELAX2)	

_____ELCS18 Answer literal questions to demonstrate comprehension of orally read age-appropriate texts. (ELAIII7)	
_____ELCS19 Respond to oral reading by commenting or questioning (ELAIII8)	
_____W16 Display or share writing samples, illustrations and dictated stories with others. (ELAVI8)	
_____W13 Record or represent and communicate observations and findings through a variety of methods (e.g. pictures, words, graphs, dramatizations) (SV8) (MII6)(MV2)	
_____S8 Ask questions about objects, organisms, *pictures, letters, signs* and events in their environment during shared stories, conversations and play (e.g., ask about how worms eat). (SV1, ELRIX1)	

_____S9 Show interest in investigating unfamiliar objects, organisms and phenomena during shared stories, conversations and play (e.g., "Where does hail come from?). (SV2)	Teacher Reflection
_____S10 Participate in simple, spontaneous scientific explorations with others (e.g., digging to the bottom of the sandbox, testing materials that sink or float). (SVI3)	Recorder: _____

* *Guidelines for ELCS Implementation* ODE 2005, rev. 2006

Standards and skills are also often documented by a child's **work sample.** This may be something created by the child or notes taken while a child engages in an activity such as "reading" a book to the teacher or his peers. These work samples are also generally identified with the standard or developmental skill evident and also placed in the child's portfolio. Documentation collected during an **investigation** is also an example of a performance-based assessment. The documentation boards items created or photos taken while engaged in tasks associated with the investigation all provide evidence of a child's knowledge and skills. This is often a part of a primary classroom as children engage in journal writing drawing of pictures or doing research with age appropriate materials.

Portfolios "Portfolios are a collection of a child's work and teacher data from informal and performance assessments to evaluate development and learning. Portfolios can be used for assessment and evaluation, for self-assessment and reflection, and for reporting progress" (Wortham, 2005, p. 205). At the early childhood level, it seems appropriate to use the portfolio as a means of assessment and evaluation and reporting progress. While children can certainly be involved in choosing which items to include in the portfolio, they are not really at a stage of development for strong self-reflection. Teachers will need to do the reflection, asking themselves "Why this item for the portfolio? What does it represent and define?" DeFina presented seven assumptions about portfolios:

- Represent a systematic effort to collect meaningful student works.
- Students should be actively involved in selecting pieces to include in the portfolio.
- Portfolios can contain materials from teachers, parents, peers, and school administrators.
- Portfolios should reflect the actual daily learning activities of children.
- Portfolios demonstrate the students' progress over time
- Portfolios may have subcomponents
- A variety of media can be used (as cited in Henniger, 1999, pp. 296-297).

Using these guidelines the teachers at the Bombeck Center have begun to develop some consistency in the organization of portfolios and are conscious of obtaining materials to document growth development and learning of content standards in the context of the daily activities. Currently teachers use a variety of documentation methods including anecdotal records and photos described above as well as samples of the child's work. Completed "Investigation Records" are also included.

Aggregating Whole Class Data

The ACCESS Class Tracking System (ACTS) is an integral part of the curriculum framework in that it captures the data that teachers collect through authentic assessment techniques onto an aggregated record that can be used in making instructional decisions (Figure 2-4). The ACTS for preschool uses a compilation of Early Learning Content Standards for English/ Language Arts, Mathematics, Science and Social Studies. Data for all children are recorded on the Content Area Specific Charts (Figure 2-5). The charts are used not only to track individual children's progress but also as a tool that informs instructional planning around a topic of investigation. Assessment tools that collect data over time and use authentic data collection techniques have been identified as preferred practice when working with young children (Mindes, 2007; Wortham, 2008).

Figure 2-5: ACCESS Curriculum Assessment System

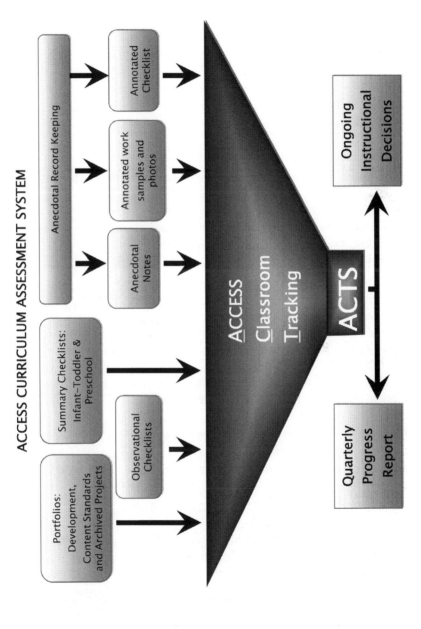

ACCESS CURRICULUM ASSESSMENT SYSTEM

Implications for Infants and Toddlers

With infants and toddlers, it can be difficult to aggregate and analyze data as a whole class when most of a teacher's time is spent caring for the basic needs of individual children. It may not be appropriate to aggregate whole class information for infants and toddlers because the program in focused on the needs of individual children. Each infant is on an individual trajectory and the curriculum for a 6 month old baby is dramatically different from a baby who is just 12 months older. Because of degree of developmental differences at this age level, aggregated data for the whole class is not as useful as it is for older children.

Using Data to Make Instructional Decisions

Collecting data through assessments is only useful if that data is then used to inform instruction. As data collection is an on-going process, with all individual data transferred onto the *ACCESS Class Tracking Sheet* (ACTS), (see figure 2-5) the teachers then use the information to focus activities and ensure all content standards are being addressed as they engage in planning for the classroom. For example, the children have expressed an interest in *worms*, and the teachers are developing the anticipatory web and collecting content specific material to engage in a investigation on worms. Numerous activities could be developed, but by looking at the tracking sheet, the teachers notice they have not worked on measurement or data analysis and probability standards. Thus, some of the activities of the investigation of worms could include measuring worms, determining similar attributes among a group of worms, or graphing the distance a worm travels in a specific period of time. All of these standards are related to the content of the investigation and allow for assessment of children's skills as they participate in performance-based assessments. Instruction may also be more focused to address a particular concept or developmental skill identified as a need through a performance assessment. This might be something related to each standard as well as processing, language, and higher order thinking skills. The principles and philosophy of the ACCESS Curriculum are appropriate for primary grades as well as for children under the age of five.

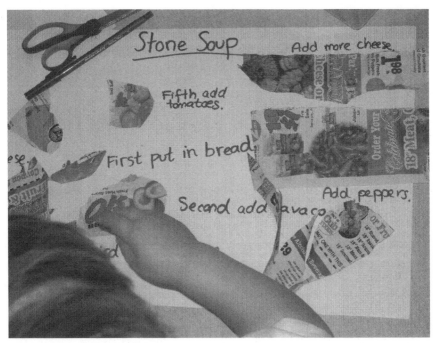

Pictures of children's work can be photographed and saved with an anecdote as evidences of an emerging or mastered skill.

This teacher is compiling information from a variety of sources onto the ACCESS Class Tracking Sheets so that she can use data to inform instruction.

Figure 2-5: ACCESS Classroom Tracking

ACCESS Classroom
Ohio Early Learning and

Language and Literacy Development

Students:	1	2	3	4	5
STRAND: Listening and Speaking					
Topic: Receptive Language and Comprehension					
Asks meaning of words					
Follows 2 step directions					
Understands complex concepts					
Understands sentences (increasing length)					
Topic: Expressive Language					
Uses language to:					
express ideas					
share observations					
problem solve					
predict					
seek information					
express ideas and feelings					
describe familiar people, places , things					
Uses drawing/visuals to support language					
Grammar:					
Uses nouns to describe					
forms regular plurals					
Understands & uses interrogatives					
Understands & uses prepositions					
Produces & expands complete sentences					
Vocabulary:					
Understands new words acquired through print					
Understands new words from variety settings					
Connects words and use					
Explores relations between word meaning					
Adapted from the Ohio Department of Education, 2013					
Topic: Social Communication					

Tracking Sheet (ACTS)
d Development Standards

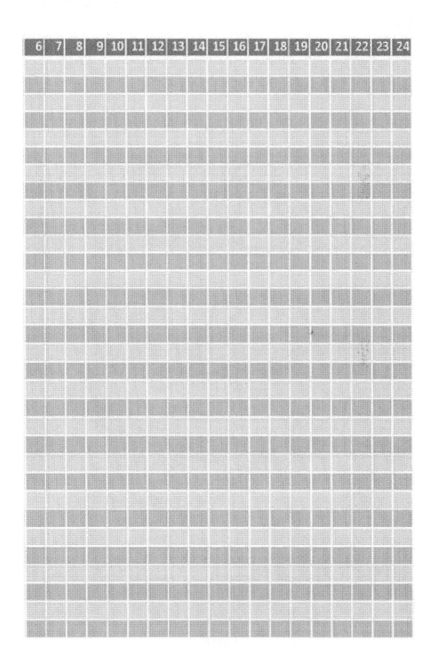

6	7	8	9	10	11	12	13	14	15	16	17	18	19	20	21	22	23	24

Teachers in primary grades are held to accountability standards, with the most notable being the beginning of high stakes testing in the 3rd grade math and reading. By carefully analyzing the performance of children, teachers can use that data to plan future activities while continuing the cycle of using assessment to inform instruction.

Application to Primary Grades

While "testing" is a more accepted tradition in primary grades (kindergarten to grade 3), many of the same principles apply to infant/toddlers or preschoolers. The principles of NAEYC and DEC/CEC continue to exist and teachers remain responsible for assessing academic content developed standards (McMillan, 2011). The federal Common Core standards in math and reading/ language arts have just recently been adopted by the federal government, and states are working on developing science and social studies standards. Most national organizations for particular content areas have standards they expect teachers to know such as the National Council of Teachers of Mathematics, as do some school systems. This results in teachers being required to "wade through" the standards to find what is appropriate for their classroom. The concept of "divide and conquer" previously discussed is a good starting place for primary teachers as well as those working at the preschool level. The standards need to be known, and be integrated to enhance learning and development of thinking skills. Learning skills in isolation has not been proven to result in long term retention (Copple & Bredekamp, 2009); however, presenting the content through an integrated unit of study/investigation provides meaning and a context for learning the required skills. Knowledge of these standards allows the teacher to determine what the students should know, leading to the first format of testing in the primary grades or pre-assessment. This is also the first step with preschool age and infant/toddlers. Is there an interest? What do they already know? How can that knowledge be built upon to further their knowledge and skills? Through developing concept maps, teachers can map the investigation in such a way to determine what the student should know, how it will be assessed, what experiences will best teach the concept, and what content standards will be addressed. McMillan (2011) calls this developing learning targets and matches the targets with an appropriate assessment. He reports a "trend of using alternative assessments" (p.15), inclusive of authentic assessments, exhibitions, portfolios, journals, and authentic assessments, with an "emphasis on authenticity" (p. 16). Many of these assessment procedures have been previously discussed, with the exception of "exhibitions" and "journals". An exhibition can be a dance, reading of a poem, completing a graph, or acting out a play. Each of these is also a performance assessment as the student is demonstrating her knowledge of the content through the exhibit. Journals can be simple or extensive. Younger children may draw pictures as they are observing a seed sprouting and growing to document changes in the seed. Older children, or those with higher developmental skills, may also draw, but add comments, measurements, or some research they have discovered. This use of a journal can cover many content standards at the appropriate grade level. See figure 2-6:

Figure 2-6

Investigation: Basic Needs of Living Things *
Standards Addressed: Living things have basic needs which are met by obtaining materials from the physical environment. * Living things survive only in environments that meet their needs. * Measure the length of an object by selecting and using appropriate tools such as rulers, yardsticks, meter sticks, and measuring tapes. Measure to determine how much longer one object is than another, expressing the length difference in terms of a standard length unit. Read with sufficient accuracy and fluency to support comprehension. a. Read grade-level text with purpose and understanding.
Experience: Students will keep a daily journal that documents change in the seed/plant. This can include drawing pictures, writing brief statements, or adding research content obtained during class time or from home.

* Ohio Science Content Standards

Teachers are encouraged to use both formative completed as the content is taught to determine knowledge level of the student and summative the total picture of what the student has learned at the end of an investigation assessments at both the preschool and primary level. Formative evaluations provide for a quick snapshot of what the student has learned in that portion of the investigation. It is used to assess learning but also to determine what to plan next. What is the next piece of content information or how can what was just learned be expanded? Teachers are encouraged to include formative assessments in their daily plans, tying instruction directly to assessment. Summative assessments provide a view of what the student has learned. This can be completed in a variety of ways; the *ACCESS* Curriculum recommends performance assessments that capture the interest of the student and allow them to demonstrate their knowledge in a variety of ways. A summative performance assessment may result in a product that reflects the awareness of simple knowledge but also a deeper understanding of the central concept of the investigation.

"High stakes testing" must be discussed when addressing learning in the primary grades. Beginning in the third grade, most students will be assessed in reading/language arts and mathematics yearly. The teachers in preschool, kindergarten, first and second grade are responsible for getting the students ready to take these tests. Third grade teachers may spend much of their time getting the students ready for the test, but research shows that through the investigative, inquiry based model of learning through the earlier years, the students are doing well on the standardized third grade tests. This requirement for having third grade students "pass" the required reading and math tests cause teachers to spend more time "teaching to the test" or teaching the format that will be used like multiple choice testing to complete the test. This is basically in direct contrast to what we know helps children learn: integration, inquiry, making knowledge meaningful, and building on prior knowledge. McMillian (2011) also discourages this model of teaching to the test and states

> It turns out that classroom assessments, especially of the formative type, that are selected and implemented on the basis of promoting student learning, rather than showing student performance, will result in higher state-level test results. The key is focusing on how classroom assessments will maximize student motivation and learning, rather than on what will result in the highest percentages of students judged at least "proficient" (p21).

Formal Assessment

As teachers work with children on a daily basis, they use their knowledge of child development and observation skills to continually assess a child's strengths and weaknesses. While all children develop at different rates, most follow predictable patterns that reflect a continual growth of skills, including from simple to complex. Occasionally, teachers notice a child who is not functioning as expected for his age, and after careful observation and documentation, determine that a more structured, formal assessment is needed. **Screening** can either be a continual process for all children or completed for an individual child based on a concern raised by a teacher or parent. For example, at the Bombeck Center, the *Ages and Stages Questionnaire* is used in the infant and toddler rooms to ensure children are developing as expected. On the preschool side, the *Brigance Early Preschool Screen-II* is completed with new students or children who appear to be having difficulties with specific aspects of development. Teachers, or others conducting the screening, must be trained to accurately administer and interpret the results and to know how to share those results with parents. Screens are used to determine if further intervention is needed and in the case of the Bombeck Center, after consulting with the parents, this probably means a referral to the local education authority or birth-to-three program. The *ACCESS Curriculum* can also be utilized as a screening tool as children can be compared to one another on the *ACCESS Class Tracking Sheet*. While this is not the primary intent of the *ACTS,* this information will be quite helpful in determining if further assistance is needed for a child.

Summary

Putting all of these pieces together, including:

- pairing standards with investigations and daily activities,
- anecdotal records and portfolio entries including pictures of children engaged in activities/play that document learning of the standards, and
- checklists that allow for quick assessing of specific skills and tracking of whole class learning,

has resulted in an assessment supported system. Teachers consider this a manageable system which allows them to use assessment data to document learning and to plan instruction. It also is a system that was helped to be created by the teachers, thus resulting in "buy-in" and use of the *ACCESS Curriculum.*

ACCESS Steps to Success: Assessment Supported Practice

Designing an Assessment System

1. Preferably before the school year begins, the teaching team identifies assessment practices that currently exist and determines the aspects of the practices that should become part of an intentional assessment system.
2. During the program evaluation process, the team identifies useful assessment data that has been collected via existing strategies. How well can these data inform instructional decisions, document child progress, and identify the interest of the children?
3. The team discusses assessment needs and preferences including how to:
    a. document child progress
    b. inform instructional decision-making
    c. document the interest of children
    d. conduct ongoing program evaluation
4. The team considers the classroom's daily routines and identifies opportunities for documenting developmental skills or early learning content standards.
5. The team considers data collection strategies including the tools provided in the *ACCESS* collection available at *www.accesscurriculum.com* and decides which tools meet the needs of the team, or if they need to modify one of the tools to fit their needs.
6. The teaching team determines the screening tool or tools to be used as children enter the program.
7. The teaching team determines who, where, when and how data will be collected.

Getting to Know Children and Families

1. The teaching team examines data that has been shared about incoming children by families, previous teachers/caregivers, and medical and school records.
2. The teaching team identifies information that still needs to be collected and selects and/or modifies tools from the *ACCESS* collection or creates their own.
3. The team screens the children. NOTE: Screening data is not used to exclude children from the program but rather as a means of informing instructional decisions.
4. The team gathers information from the family through a detailed application, introductory survey, center-based intake interview and/or home-based intake interview.

Compiling Data

1. The team compiles initial data about children using either the hard copy or electronic version of the *ACCESS* Class Tracking Sheets (ACTS) available in the *ACCESS* collection at *www.accesscurriculum.com*
2. As new data is collected, the team updates the ACTS to reflect current information on the progress and interests of children.

Analyzing and Reflecting on Data

1. The team meets weekly to discuss assessment data as part of the instructional planning process.
2. The team uses data to make instructional decisions, to track progress of individual children and the class as a whole, to identify the interests of children, and to evaluate program effectiveness.
3. The team determines what data needs to be collected in the future and adds or deletes tools as needed.

4. The team reflects on data collection processes and adjusts who, when, where, and how data is being collected as needed.

Sharing Progress with Families

1. The team shares information about child progress and interests with families using classroom-based or electronic portfolios, document boards, informal conversation, and formal conferences during quarterly progress report meetings.
2. The team determines how social media and web sites might be used to facilitate information sharing with families. See *www.accesscurriculum.com* for social media safety information.
3. The team determines an ongoing process to share important program philosophies and early childhood research-based practice with families. For example:
   a. Kindergarten readiness is not an event but rather a process that begins in utero.
   b. Developmentally appropriate and play-based practice is the best way to grow the brain and get children ready for kindergarten and later school success.

The Transition Process

1. The team develops a transition process that facilitates information sharing with programs that are receiving children from your program.
2. The team selects, revises or develops transitions documents that share information with programs that are receiving children from your program.
3. The team identifies and/or plans opportunities to visit and/or learn about program options so that families can make informed decisions.

References

Bagnato, S. J., Neisworth, J. T., & Munson, S. M. (1997). *LINKing assessment and early intervention: An authentic curriculum-based approach.* Baltimore, MD: Paul H. Brookes Publishing.

Baldwin, J. L., Adams, S. M., & Kelly, M. K. (2009). Science at the center: An emergent, standards-based, child-centered framework for early learners. *Early Childhood Education Journal, 37,* 71-77.

Beaty, J. J. (2013). *Observing development of the young child* (8th ed.). Columbus, OH: Merrill Prentice Hall.

Henniger, M. L. (1999). *Teaching young children: An introduction.* Upper Saddle River, NJ: Merrill Prentice Hall.

Linder, T. (2008). *Administration guide for TPBA 2 & TPBI 2.* Baltimore: Paul H. Brookes Publishing Co.

Meisels, S. J., & Atkins-Burnett, S. (2000). The elements of early childhood assessment. In J. P. Shonkoff & S. J. Meisels (Eds.), *Handbook of early childhood intervention* (2nd ed., pp. 231-257). New York: Cambridge University Press.

Mindes, G. (2007). *Assessing young children.* (3rd ed.). Upper Saddle River, NJ: Pearson/Merrill/Prentice Hall.

National Association for the Education of Young Children and the National Association of Early Childhood Specialists in State Departments of Education. (2003). *Early childhood curriculum, assessment, and program evaluation: Building an effective, accountable system in programs for children birth through age 8* [Joint position statement]. Washington DC: National Association for the Education of Young Children.

Neisworth, J. T., & Bagnato, S. J. (2004). The mismeasure of young children: The authentic assessment alternative. *Infants and Young Children, 17*(3), 198-212.

Ohio Department of Education. (2004). *Early learning content standards.* Columbus, OH: Author.

Worthham, S. C. (2005). *Assessment in early childhood education* (5th). Upper Saddle River, NJ: Pearson/Merrill/Prentice Hall.

Whether, social, emotional, cognitive or physical development and learning, ACCESS provides opportunities to meet the needs of children throughout each day.

3

Child-Centered Practice

ACCESS adheres to the notion of child-centeredness's complexity and "focuses more on the importance of children's individual interests and their freedom to create their own learning through choosing from various classroom activities" Tzuo, 2007, p 33.

ACCESS is based on a child-centered approach to curriculum that encourages teachers to provide opportunities for children to solve their own problems and be responsible for many of their own achievements. Based on a belief that child-centered practice follows the needs of children, *ACCESS* recognizes the importance of teacher support and direction as well as child-directed experiences. As Honig (2010) suggests, there are times when a bit of teacher intervention may be just the right thing:

> Children can accomplish some tasks on their own after trying hard. Others are too easy or too difficult. Children get restless and bored when toys or tasks are too easy. They feel frustrated when tasks are too challenging. The Russian child-development theorist Vygotsky taught that teachers are priceless in supporting child learning and accomplishment when a task is just a bit too difficult at the child's present level of development. Then a teaching adult provides just that bit of help that will result in further child learning and satisfaction. Vygotsky used the term "zone of proximal development" for the difference between what a child can do on his or her own compared with what the child can do with adult help. With the assistance of an adult, a child will be able to succeed at a cognitive or social learning task beyond what he or she could have accomplished alone.

Because of a sound grounding in the traditional early childhood theory base and current research in the field, *ACCESS* places a high value in child-centered practice by being intentional in how teachers and children interact, how the environment is staged, how materials are selected and how play is supported to inspire learning and development.

Child-centered practice is synonymous with quality for many early childhood professionals; however, the meaning of the phrase varies as over 40 definitions have appeared in the literature starting with Froebel in 1778 (Chung and Walsh, 2000; Tzuo, 2007). The term, in one of its simplest interpretations, encourages a curriculum that focuses on the interests of children. It is often contrasted with teacher-directed approaches that give the control for content and selection of materials and activities to the teacher. *ACCESS* adheres to the notion of child-centeredness as complex and "focuses more on the importance of children's individual interests and their freedom to create their own learning through choosing from various classroom activities. In contrast, teacher-directed curriculum places more stress on the teacher's control over children's exploration of learning" (Tzuo, 2007, p33). *ACCESS* is based on research that indicates a child-centered curriculum can benefit children's school progress and personal adjustment (Dunn & Kontos, 1997; Frede & Barnett, 1992; Hirsh-Pasek, Hyson, & Rescorla, 1990). *ACCESS* adheres to the following principles.

ACCESS Principles for a Child-centered Curriculum

- Curriculum is age appropriate and avoids push-down models.
- Curriculum reflects an understanding of development and learning.
- Curriculum respects and reflects family culture.
- Curriculum provides opportunities for high quality teacher-child and child to child interaction.
- Environments support active and/or play-based learning in all domains of development at all ages birth through age eight.
- Teachers rely on authentic materials which are readily available throughout a carefully designed classroom environment.
- Classroom environments are designed to support active, integrated, inquiry-based child-centered learning.
- All children/students have access to rich, challenging and engaging curriculum.

For many, child-centered practice and developmentally appropriate practice are closely related if not synonymous. By using documentation to support decisions, *ACCESS* incorporates NAEYC' s (2009) emphasis of intentionality. As a framework that is supported by assessment, *ACCESS* allows teachers to make informed and intentional decisions about instruction which take into consideration the interests of the children in the classroom and also the children's need to be active, to make choices and to play.

When making curriculum decisions, teachers who use *ACCESS* base their instructional decisions on the core considerations of developmentally appropriate practice such as:

1. What is known about child development and learning? Are the teachers knowledgeable concerning children's age-related characteristics thus permitting general predictions about what experiences are likely to promote their learning and development?
2. What is known about each child as an individual? What have practitioners learned about each child that has implications for how best to adapt and be responsive to that individual variation?
3. What is known about the social and cultural contexts in which children live? Is the staff familiar with the values, expectations, and behavioral and linguistic conventions that shape children's lives in their homes and communities which will then help to ensure that learning experiences in the program or school are meaningful, relevant and respectful for each child and family (NAEYC, 2009, p. 9-10)?

Child-centered Curriculum is Age Appropriate

When planning curriculum and the environments that support development and learning, *ACCESS* asks teachers to have a firm understanding of the implications of the 12 Principles of Development and Learning as stated in NAEYC's *Developmentally Appropriate Practice in Early Childhood Programs: Serving Children from Birth through Age 8* (2009). These principles are the basis for age appropriate practice for children ages birth through age 8, and teachers need to be able to apply these principles in a variety of situations. For many early childhood professionals, rereading these principals will be a refresher of coursework and/or professional development that addresses the professional knowledge base known as child development. For those who are new to the field and are unfamiliar with child development and the NAEYC Principles of Development and Learning, additional study of this vitally important content is warranted.

The 12 Principles of Development and Learning

The NAEYC (2009) has identified the following principles as the basis of quality experiences:

1. All the domains of development and learning-physical, social and emotional, and cognitive—are important, and they are closely interrelated. Children's development and learning in one domain influence and are influenced by what takes place in other domains.
2. Many aspects of children's learning and development follow well documented sequences with later abilities, skills, and knowledge building on those already acquired.
3. Development and learning proceed at varying rates from child to child as well as at uneven rates across different areas of a child's individual functioning.
4. Development and learning result from a dynamic and continuous interaction of biological maturation and experience.
5. Early experiences have profound effects, both cumulative and delayed, on a child's development and learning; and optimal periods exist for certain types of development and learning to occur.
6. Development proceeds toward greater complexity, self-regulation and symbolic or representational capacities.
7. Children develop best when they have secure, consistent relationships with responsive adults and opportunities for positive relationships with peers.
8. Development and learning occur in and are influenced by multiple social and cultural contexts.
9. Children learn in a variety of ways; a wide range of teaching strategies and interactions are effective in supporting all these kinds of learning.
10. Play is an important vehicle for developing self-regulation as well as for promoting language, cognition and social competence.
11. Development and learning advance when children are challenged to achieve at a level just beyond their current mastery, and also when they have many opportunities to practice newly acquired skills.
12. Children's experiences help develop persistence, initiative, and flexibility; in turn, these dispositions and behaviors affect their motivation, learning and development.
    (Adapted from the National Association for the Education of Young Children Position Statement on Developmentally Appropriate Practice, 2009, pp. 11-16).

In addition to the broader principles of development and learning, *ACCESS* also requires that teachers have a sound understanding of developmental and academic skills that are consistent with the ages of children served in their classroom.

Infants and toddlers in programs using the ACCESS Curriculum benefit from a curriculum that supports development across all domains.

Infant and Toddler Development

Teachers at the Bombeck Family Learning Center who work with infants and toddlers have a deep understanding and ability to support *Ohio's Infant and Toddler Guidelines* (Ohio Child Care Resource and Referral Agency, 2006). These guidelines were developed by a group of early childhood stakeholders under the coordination of the Ohio Child Care Resource and Referral Agency and the Ohio Department of Jobs and Family Services and are considered to be a model nationally for infant and toddler developmental expectations. The complete and very detailed document can be found at *http://jfs.ohio.gov/cdc/infanttoddler.pdf.* An overview of what is included in these guidelines is depicted in figure 3-1.

Figure 3-1: Ohio Infant and Toddler Guidelines (2006) Six Developmental Domains

---

The Six Developmental Domains at the Heart of School and Life Success

Physical Health
Physical health is optimal when safe health practices and nutrition are combined with nurturing and responsive caregiving. Protecting children from illness and injury, and providing them with individually appropriate nutrition and a sanitary environment that reduces the risk of infectious disease, is important for all caregivers.

Language and Communication Development
Language and communication development is the increasing ability to communicate successfully with others to build relationships, share meaning and express needs in multiple ways.

Social Development
Social development is the child's emerging development of an understanding of self and others, and the ability to relate to other people and the environment.

Emotional Development
Emotional development is the child's emerging ability to become secure, express feelings, develop self-awareness and self-regulate.

Motor Development
Motor development is the increasing ability to use one's body to interact with the environment.

Cognitive Development
Cognitive development is the building of thinking skills.

Adapted from the *Ohio Infant and Toddler Guidelines: Early Experiences Last a Lifetime,* Ohio Child Care Resource and Referral Agency, 2006, p. ii.

Preschool teachers follow the children's lead to support development by being aware of their interests.

Preschool Development

Preschool teachers using *ACCESS* must also be well versed in the development and learning that can be expected for children ages three through five. *ACCESS* is committed to supporting development across all domains and also includes early learning content. While teachers can use the developmental and learning standards that have been adopted by their state or program, one set of national standards to be considered is the Head Start Child Development and Early Learning Framework It is a model that is comprehensive in its attention to all developmental domains (see figure 3-2). Many states, including Ohio, have used the Head Start Child Development and Early Learning Framework as a model because of its thoughtful and comprehensive inclusion of domains of development (see figure 3-2). *Developmentally Appropriate Practice in Early Childhood Programs: Serving Children from Birth through Age 8* (Copple and Bredekamp, 2009).

Figure 3-2: The Head Start Child Development and Early Learning Framework

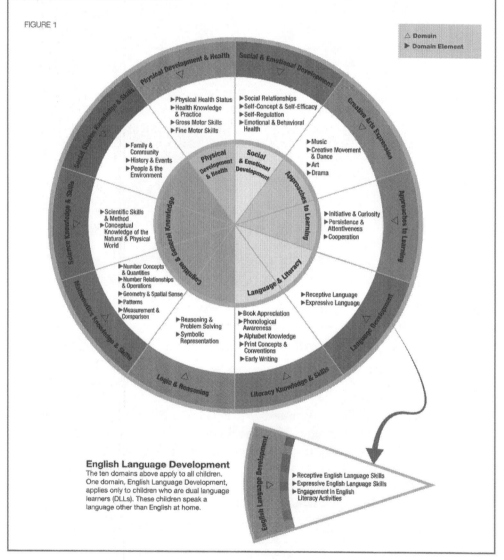

The Head Start Child Development and Early Learning Framework
Promoting Positive Outcomes in Early Childhood Programs Serving Children 3-5 Years Old

The *Framework* represents the foundation of the Head Start Approach to School Readiness. It aligns with and builds from the five essential domains of school readiness identified by the National Education Goals Panel (see inner circle) and lays out essential areas of learning and development. The *Framework* can be used to guide curriculum, implementation, and assessment to plan teaching and learning experiences that align to school readiness goals and track children's progress across developmental domains. The domains △ and domain elements ▶ apply to all 3 to 5 year olds in Head Start and other early childhood programs, including dual language learners and children with disabilities.

Like preschool practice, child-centered programming for children in kindergarten and the primary grades focuses on developmental skills and academic content.

Development of Children in Kindergarten and the Primary Grades

Early childhood includes children ages birth through age 8. Despite this well recognized age range, it is common for the focus of development to center on infants, toddlers and preschoolers. *ACCESS* in kindergarten and the primary grades is dependent on a sound understanding of the developmental tendencies that comprise this unique stage of the human life cycle. It is important that teachers are well grounded in developmental skills appropriate for the age of the children in their classroom. Figure 3-3 provides an overview of developmental skills that can serve as a refresher for early childhood trained teachers. If this information is foreign to you, consider learning more by taking coursework, participating in professional development and consulting the child development resources listed at the end of this chapter.

Figure 3-3 Selected Developmental Skills for Children in Kindergarten and the Primary Grades

Emotional Development	**Social Development**
• Seeks adult approval for efforts (7 years) • Wants to go to school. Seems disappointed if he/she must miss (8 years) • Handles stressful situations without becoming overly upset or aggressive (8 years)	• Engages in cooperative play with other children; participates in group decisions, role assignments and rule observance (6 years) • Makes friends easily (7 years) • Participates in some group activities (8 years) • Interacts and plays cooperatively with other children (8 years)
Cognitive Development	**Approaches to Learning**
• Sorts objects on one or more dimensions (6 years) • Shows understanding of some cause and effect concepts (8 years) • Knows how to tell time (8 years) • Counts by rote to 10; knows what number comes next (8 years)	• Concentrates on completing puzzles and board games (7 years) • Plans and carries out simple projects with minimal adult help (7 years) • Carries out multiple four or five step instructions (8 years)
Language/Literacy Development	**Aesthetic Development**
• Carries on conversations using complex sentences (6 years) • Uses all grammatical structures; pronouns, plurals, verb tenses, conjunctions (7 years) • Names most letters and numerals (6 years) • Copies his or her own first name (6 years) • Expresses complex thoughts in a clear and logical fashion (8 years) • Reads and comprehends a story (8 years)	• Shows interest in creative expression (8 years)

Physical and Health Development	Motor Development
• Continues to grow in height and weight (7 years) • Sleeps undisturbed through the night (7 years) • Has energy to play (8 years) • Has a good appetite. Shows interest in eating new foods (8 years) • Has few illnesses (8 years)	*Gross Motor Skills* • Skips with alternating feet (6 years) • Hops for several seconds on one foot (6 years) *Fine Motor Skills* • Cuts out simple shapes (6 years) • Ties his or her shoes (7 years) • Demonstrates consistent right or left handedness (8 years) • Uses a pencil in a deliberate and controlled manner (8 years) • Uses eating utensils with ease (8 years)

Marotz and Allen, 2013, pp. 268-270

The Importance of Play

Play is the work of childhood, and it provides fertile ground for development and learning. *ACCESS* provides children with an intellectually engaging curriculum and believes an important vehicle for learning and development is play. *ACCESS* recognizes that children learn best when engaged, and play is the medium that is most highly engaging. In its 2009 position statement, NAEYC states that: "Play is an important vehicle for children's social, emotional, and cognitive development, as well as a reflection of their development."

Play is the foundation of a well-constructed early childhood curriculum, and it is vital that the teachers stage the environment to support children in their play. Intentional teachers have a good understanding of the types of play that each of the children in the class engage in. We recommend that this understanding be informed by documentation collected on children overtime. Figure 3-4: *Assessment of Play* is a tool that many ACCESS teachers use to assess play so that the environment can be appropriately staged and play can be supported.

Figure 3-4: Assessment of Play

ASSESSMENT OF PLAY

Children	Cognitive Dimensions of Play			
	Functional Play: Repetitive action that children enjoy.	**Constructive Play:** Using blocks, art supplies, beads, recycled objects and even sand to create or build.	**Dramatic Play:** Using the imagination to create or recreate stories from the children's personal life experience or from make-believe.	**Games with Rules:** Begins to emerge at around age five when children have the cognitive and social skills to value a play experience with structured rules even though they may not win.
1				
2				
3				
4				
5				
6				
7				
8				
9				
10				
11				
12				
13				
14				
15				
16				
17				
18				
19				
20				
21				

Children	Social Dimensions of Play					
	Unoccupied: Not engaged in play.	**Solitary:** The child plays alone and independently even if surrounded by other children.	**Onlooker:** The child watches other children or adults play. May engage in conversation but not engaged in the play.	**Parallel:** The child is aware of peers but plays independently at the same activity, at the same time, and in the same place as another child or children.	**Associative:** The child is still focused on a separate activity but there is a considerable amount of sharing, lending, taking turns, and attending to the activities of one's peers.	**Cooperative:** The child engages in high levels of play in which 2 or more children organize their play and/or activity cooperatively with a common goal and are able to differentiate and assign roles.
1						
2						
3						
4						
5						
6						
7						
8						
9						
10						
11						
12						
13						
14						
15						
16						
17						
18						
19						
20						
21						

Teachers may assume that they already know how children play in their classroom. We have found that intentionally collecting data about children's play provides consistent data and a more complete picture of opportunities for social and cognitive development. Teachers often overestimate their ability to keep track of this information. Once teachers understand how their children engage in social and cognitive play, they can stage the environment differently or provide support that encourages children to grow.

The Environment as Teacher

ACCESS views the classroom environment as vital in creating an inspiring child-centered curriculum. An organized and well-staged environment will support learning in all domains of development; will inspire wonder, creativity and innovation; and will help children organize their neuro-network to make sense of their world. With *ACCESS*, the physical environment must be intentionally designed to support the strengths, needs and interests of the children in the room both individually and collectively. The environment is not static and evolves as the children grow and develop and as their interests change.

ACCESS relies on sound research in the design and arrangement of the classroom environment. Teachers and teaching teams conduct self-assessments of the environment using the *Infant Toddler Environment Rating Scale—Revised* (ITERS-R) (Harms, T, Clifford, R.M., & Cryer, D., 2006); the *Early Childhood Environment Rating Scale-Revised* (ECERS-R) (Clifford, R.M., Cryer, D., & Harms, T, 2004); or the *Classroom Environment Self-Assessment: Kindergarten-Primary* (CESA: K-P) (see figure 3-5) and identify areas of strength and goals for the classroom environment.

When staging the environment, teaching teams must be familiar with age appropriate development of the children in the classroom. They must get to know the families of the children and gather information about family culture that will inform child-centered experiences.

Once ACCESS teachers have a sound understanding of the children and families, they will arrange the classroom in a manner that reflects the strengths, needs and interests of the children, the family cultures, and the results of the classroom environment self-assessments. Environments are not static, and the teaching team must reevaluate and adjust the environment to support development and learning throughout the year. Because environments reflect the children in the classroom, it is likely that if the program consists of more than one classroom, the designs, arrangement and materials will be unique.

Indoor and out-of-door environments support development across all domains for children of all ages.

Figure 3-5 Classroom Environment Self-Assessment: Kindergarten-Primary
(CESA: K-P)

TARGET	DESCRIPTION OF CURRENT PRACTICE AND GOALS FOR IMPROVEMENT
A. Classroom Climate	
1. The classroom establishes and maintains an atmosphere of respect, inclusivity and tolerance.	
2. Classroom rules and consequences are established cooperatively by both the teacher and the children at the beginning of the school year.	
3. The meaning and implication of classroom rules are taught on an ongoing basis until all children understand both the rules and the consequences.	
4. Techniques such as the "morning meeting" are used to build classroom community, understand citizenship and discuss issues as they arise.	
B. Classroom Design	
1. The classroom design supports executive functioning by highlighting items to be attended to and minimizing visual clutter.	
2. The classroom is used as a vehicle that supports aesthetic development by attending to color, light, pattern and space.	
3. Ideally, classrooms have windows and ample natural light. Artificial light is conducive to comfort and learning.	
4. Documentation (bulletin) boards are learning tools that intentionally communicate what the children are learning.	

5. Natural and authentic objects are present for children to explore as they develop a sense of beauty.	
C. Classroom Arrangement	
1. The arrangement includes clearly defined spaces that communicate the purpose of the space and foster easy movement throughout the classroom.	
2. The arrangement allows for child directed and teacher directed instruction.	
3. The arrangement allows for whole class, flexible small group, paired and individual learning.	
4. The arrangement provides tables/ desks and chairs that appropriately fit each child in the classroom.	
5. The arrangement provides a safe space for children to develop organizational structures as they store their belongings.	
6. The arrangement provides a carpeted open area for floor work, story reading, and stretching allowing children to be comfortable for extended periods.	
7. The arrangement provides shelving and display space that showcases the materials that are currently in use.	
8. The arrangement includes hidden storage for materials that are not in use.	
9. The arrangement supports active and/ or play-based learning in all domains of development.	
10. The arrangement provides a welcoming and comfortable space for adults including the teaching team, volunteers, observers and families.	

Authentic Materials

In *ACCESS*, materials selection is intentional and reflects the strengths, needs and interests of the children. With other curriculums, materials might be bought at the beginning of the year for all of the classrooms. This one size fits all approach is not consistent with the *ACCESS* curriculum. Intentional selection of materials requires that teachers understand the prior knowledge of children and choose materials that are safe but realistic. As a guide for teachers in materials selection, we have provided a tool entitled, the *Continuum of Authenticity*, (see figure 3-6) which is used to evaluate how engaged children are likely to be with the materials provided. With the exception of quality fiction and nonfiction children's literature, which should be abundant and accessible for children, ACCESS classrooms should have more 3 dimensional true-to-life materials. ACCESS requires that teachers select authentic materials that will support exploration, inquiry, learning, development and play.

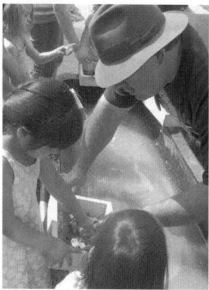

Figure 3-6 Continuum of Authenticity

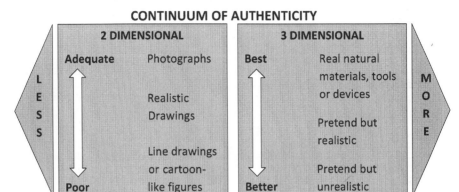

The organization of key materials is intentional and considers how objects are highlighted by their placement in the classroom. Only materials that are currently in use are present in the classroom, and storage of materials is attractive and includes cues for children so that they can easily return them to their proper place. The location of materials encourages children to use all spaces in the room. For example, dramatic play figures might be included in the block area to encourage those who ordinarily don't engage in block play to use that center. Materials are rotated to reflect the current curriculum, and unused materials are stored out of site to reduce visual clutter.

Accessible to all Children

All children have access to a rich, challenging and engaging curriculum. Many materials are open-ended and can be used in different ways by children with a variety of strengths, needs and interests. Whether differences are due to variations in age, gender, ability or family culture, teachers stage the environment, support play and make accommodations or modifications that make the curriculum accessible for all children.

Child-centered and Teacher Directed

Many of the decisions made by teachers using *ACCESS* are teacher-directed *and* based on assessment data that provides information about individual children's developmental and academic levels as well as their areas of interest. Teachers are also expected to be aware of the children's family and cultural backgrounds and the early learning content standards that have been adopted by the state in which they teach. Equipped with the data that they need to make informed decisions, teachers determine how the classroom environment is staged, what authentic materials are included and what experiences, both child-directed and teacher-directed, will be planned. Teachers use these same data to determine the topics of investigations that are most beneficial for this particular group of children. For example:

Two teachers were working with preschoolers during dramatic play in a preschool classroom. They saw that the children were intensely interested in styling hair and had created a beauty parlor in the housekeeping area. They also saw another group of children in the block area creating roads for toy trucks. They began to document both play scenarios and found that both groups of children were using rich language and a well-developed sense of story. They began to consider how they might capitalize on these areas of interest.

Looking back at the assessment data that was aggregated for the whole class, the teachers found that the children were in the midst of recognizing print in the environment and that many could benefit from the experience of creating signs and labels to inform others. This would also support letter recognition and phonemic awareness. The teachers also noted that they had not addressed any of the social studies content standards related to economics such as scarcity and resource allocation, production, consumption and distribution and could do more with geography and maps. They also saw that there was a need to explore more physical science. In looking at their data on development, they found that the boys and girls were becoming increasingly segregated in their play which was resulting in issues with classroom community. Several of the children had needs in fine motor skills related to pencil control and cutting with scissors.

As they considered these data, the teachers expressed concern that the beauty parlor, while interesting to a group of children, did not, in this situation, support safe opportunities for problem solving and investigation. Choosing the "beauty parlor" as a topic for investigation would likely exasperate the gender divide that was developing in the classroom. Instead, the teachers decided to entice children into an investigation on building a town. Both roads and the beauty parlor could be incorporated as could the other stores and services needed for people in the town. There could be a focus on construction which could include physical science as well as engineering. The children could determine signage for the town which would support purposeful and connected literacy.

As the details of this investigation emerged, it was apparent that the intentionality of the ACCESS planning process was based on elements of both child-directed and teacher-directed learning.

Addressing Content Standards in a Child-centered Curriculum

The ACCESS Curriculum Framework is systematic in that teachers use an assessment system to inform instructional decisions that meet the needs of children. The planning process is also systematic in that it is based on extended investigations of topics interesting to this particular group of children. Experiences are planned to lead to deeper understanding of the topic of investigation, and the manner in which materials are presented often reflects what children know and are able to do or what they are ready to work on next based on a review of the assessment data. The planning process allows teachers to be intentional as they facilitate children's investigations by providing them with a way to systematically collect and organize assessment data in order to make informed decisions about instruction. Consider this example:

A group of children found an intricate web that a spider was building on the classroom window frame. The children began to make observations about what they saw, and their interest was consistent. The children entered the classroom each morning and gathered at the window to see what the spider had constructed. After consulting with the teaching team and brainstorming various directions that an investigation on spiders might take, the teacher referred to the class assessment data to decide how to guide the start of the children's investigation. The teacher noted that many of the children needed more experiences with using drawings to communicate meaning, so she presented them each with a science journal in which they could draw their observation of what they saw each morning. She knew that presenting a collection of nonfiction picture books about spiders in close proximity to the window would likely inspire the children to research what they saw using the books. The assessment data also showed that many of the children were ready to demonstrate that writing has a purpose. She provided a box of note cards on the table and modeled how children could reproduce spider pictures and/or the names of spiders that were shown in the books. After a while, the children discovered that the spider was a Black and Yellow Garden Spider and its web was called an orb web. The collection of cards grew as they captured what they learned in their research.

This example demonstrates how an investigation that emanates from the interest of the children can be approached systematically when assessment data is collected and organized.

Chapter Summary

Child-centered instruction is complex and requires that the teacher is well informed about child development and is able to collect documentation about children's developmental skills and interests. This documentation is used to make decisions about how to stage environments, how to choose authentic materials and when to incorporate teacher directed instruction. Play is an important teaching strategy that is vital to learning for children ages birth through age eight. Supporting play is difficult as many teachers want to either take a hands-off approach or become too directive. ACCESS stresses the importance of following the child's lead as the teacher's role in play.

ACCESS Steps to Success:
Child-centered Practice

1. Conduct a self-assessment of the environment using the *Infant Toddler Environment Rating Scale—Revised* (ITERS-R) (Harms,T, Clifford, R.M., & Cryer, D., 2006); the *Early Childhood Environment Rating Scale-Revised* (ECERS-R) (Clifford, R.M., Cryer, D., & Harms, T, 2004); or the *Classroom Environment Self-Assessment: Kindergarten-Primary* (CESA: K-P) (Adams, Baldwin, Comingore and Kelly, 2013, p.) and identify areas of strength and goals for the classroom environment.

2. Be familiar with age appropriate development of the children in your classroom.

3. Get to know the families of the children and gather information about family culture that will inform child-centered experiences.

4. Observe children to become familiar with their individual strengths, needs and interests.

5. Use the "Assessment of Play" checklist to gain understanding of the types of social and cognitive play present in your classroom. Reevaluate play and adjust your environment throughout the year.

6. Arrange your classroom considering the needs of your children and the results of the self-assessment of your environment. Reevaluate and adjust the environment to support development and learning throughout the year.

7. Select authentic materials that will support exploration, inquiry, language and concept development and play.

8. Place materials in the classroom in such a way that they are highlighted, and provide cues for appropriate storage.

9. Rotate materials to reflect the current curriculum, and store unused materials out of sight to reduce visual clutter.

10. Support children's play without directing it.

11. Be intentional about when teacher directed experiences are used.

12. Analyze and interpret assessment data/documentation when planning experiences that meet the children's learning and developmental needs.

13. Incorporate the interests of children as well as their questions in classroom experiences.

Child Development Resources

Books:

Beaty, J.J. (2013). *Observing the development of the young child.* Upper Saddle River, NJ: Pearson Education.

Copple, C. & Bredecamp, S. (Eds). (2009).*Developmentally appropriate practice in early childhood programs: Serving children from birth to age 8* (3rd ed.). Washington DC: National Association for the Education of Young Children.

Marotz, L.R. & Allen, K.E. (2013). *Developmental profiles: Pre-birth through adolescence.* Belmont, CA: Wadsworth Cengage Learning.

Ohio Child Care Resource and Referral Agency. (2006). *Ohio's infant and toddler guidelines: Early experiences last a lifetime.* Columbus, OH: Author. Retrieved 7/12/13 from http://jfs.ohio.gov/cdc/infanttoddler.pdf.

Wortham, S. C. (2010). *Early childhood curriculum: Developmental bases for learning and teaching* (5th ed.). Upper Saddle River, NJ: Prentice Hall.

Websites:

Association for Childhood Education International
　　http://www.acei.org/programs-events/global-summit-on-childhood/page-3.html
Center on the Developing Child at Harvard University
　　http://developingchild.harvard.edu/
Division of Early Childhood-Council for Exceptional Children
　　http://www.dec-sped.org/
Medline Plus
　　http://www.nlm.nih.gov/medlineplus/childdevelopment.html
National Association for the Education of Young Children
　　http://naeyc.org/
Ohio's Infant and Toddler Guidelines: Early Experiences Last a Lifetime. http://jfs.ohio.gov/cdc/infanttoddler.pdf.
Pathways.org
　　http://www.pathways.org/top/who-is-pathways#.UeK_s42xeSo
Ready Set Soar 5 to Thrive Readiness Check-up
　　http://www.fivetothrivedayton.org/index.php?page=readiness-check-up

The Head Start Child Development and Early Learning Framework: Promoting Positive Outcomes in Early Childhood Programs Serving Children 3-5 Years Old
http://eclkc.ohs.acf.hhs.gov/hslc/tta-system/teaching/eecd/ Assessment/Child%20Outcomes/HS_Revised_Child_Outcomes_ Framework(rev-Sept2011).pdf
Zero to Three
http://www.zerotothree.org/

References

Adams, S.M., Comingore, J.L. and Baldwin, J.L. (2011). *ACCESS Curriculum Framework Implementation Guide.* Bloomington, IN: Xlibris.

Baldwin, J.L., Adams, S.M., & Kelly, M.K. (2009). Science at the center: An emergent, standards-based, child-centered framework for early learners. *Early Childhood Education Journal, 37*(2), 71-77.

Camilli, G., Vargas, S., Ryan, S., & Barnett, W.S. (2010). Meta-analysis of the effects of early education interventions on cognitive and social development. *Teachers College Record* Volume 112, Number 3, March 2010, pp. 579-620.

Chung S, Walsh DJ (2000). Unpacking child-centeredness: A history of meanings. Curric. Stud., 32: 215-234. Cooper, J.L., Masi, R., & Vick, J. (2009). *Social-emotional development in early childhood: What every policymaker should know.* New York: National Center for Children in Poverty.

Clifford, R.M., Cryer, D. & Harms, T. (2006). *Infant toddler environment rating scale.* Revised. New York: Teachers College Press.

Copple, C. & Bredecamp, S. (Eds). (2009). *Developmentally appropriate practice in early childhood programs: Serving children from birth to age 8* (3rd ed.). Washington DC: National Association for the Education of Young Children.

Dunn, L. & Kontos, S. (1997). What have we learned about developmentally appropriate practice? *Young Children,* 52, 4-13.

Ewing Marion Kaufmann Foundation (2002). Set for success: Building a strong foundation for school readiness based on social-emotional development of young children. *Kaufman Early Education Exchange, 1*(1), 1-100.

File, N. K., & Kontos, S. (1993). The relationship of program quality to children's play in integrated early intervention settings. *Topics in Early Childhood Special Education, 13,* 1-18.

Frede, E. and Ackerman, (2007). Preschool curriculum decision-making: Dimensions to consider. *Preschool Policy Brief.* 12. Brunswick, NJ: National Institute for Early Education Research.

Frede, E. & Barnett, W.S. (1992). Developmentally appropriate public school preschool: A study of implementation of the High/Scope curriculum and its effects on disadvantaged children's skills at first grade. *Early Childhood Research Quarterly, 7*(4), 483-499.

Harms, T., Clifford, R.M., & Cryer, D. (2006). *Early childhood environment rating scale.* Revised. New York: Teachers College Press.

Head Start Resource Center (2010). *The Head Start child development and early learning framework promoting positive outcomes in early childhood programs serving children 3-5 years old.* Arlington, VA: Office of Head Start, Administration for Children and Families, U.S. Department of Health and Human Services.

Hirsh-Pasek, Hyson, & Rescorla, 1990 Academic environments in preschool: Do they pressure or challenge young children? *Early Education and Development, 1*(6), 401-423.

Honig, A.S. (2010). *Little Kids, Big Worries: Stress-Busting Tips for Early Childhood Classrooms.* Baltimore, MD: Brookes Publishing.

Howes, C., & Smith, E. W. (1995). Relations among child care quality, teacher behavior, children's play activities, emotional security, and cognitive activity in child care. *Early Childhood Research Quarterly, 10*(4), 381-404.

National Scientific Council on the Developing Child. (2007). *The science of early childhood development.* Cambridge, MA: Harvard University. (Retrieved 11/16/2011) http://www.developingchild.net.

Ohio Child Care Resource and Referral Agency. (2006). *Ohio's Infant and Toddler Guidelines: Early Experiences Last a Lifetime.* Columbus, OH: Author. Retrieved 7/12/13 from http://jfs.ohio.gov/cdc/infanttoddler.pdf.

Parten, M. (1932). Social participation among preschool children. *Journal of Abnormal and Social Psychology, 27,* 243-269.

Peth-Pierce, R. (2001). *A good beginning: Sending America's children to school with the social emotional competence they need to succeed.* Child Mental Health Foundations and Agencies Network (FAN) Monograph. Bethesda, MD: National Institute of Mental Health, Office of Communications and Public Liaison.

Piaget, J. (1962). *Play, dreams, and imitation in childhood.* New York: W.W. Norton & Co.

Raver, C.C. (2002). *Emotions matter: Making the case for the role of young children's emotional development for early school readiness.* Ann Arbor, MI: Society for Research in Child Development.

Smilansky, S. (1968). *The effects of sociodramatic play on disadvantaged preschool children.* New York: Wiley.

Tzuo, P.W. (2007). The tension between teacher control and children's freedom in a child-centered classroom: Resolving the practical dilemma through a closer look at the related theories. *Early Childhood Education Journal*, Vol. 35, No. 1.

Wortham, S. C. (2010). *Early childhood curriculum: Developmental bases for learning and teaching* (5th ed.). Upper Saddle River, NJ: Prentice Hall.

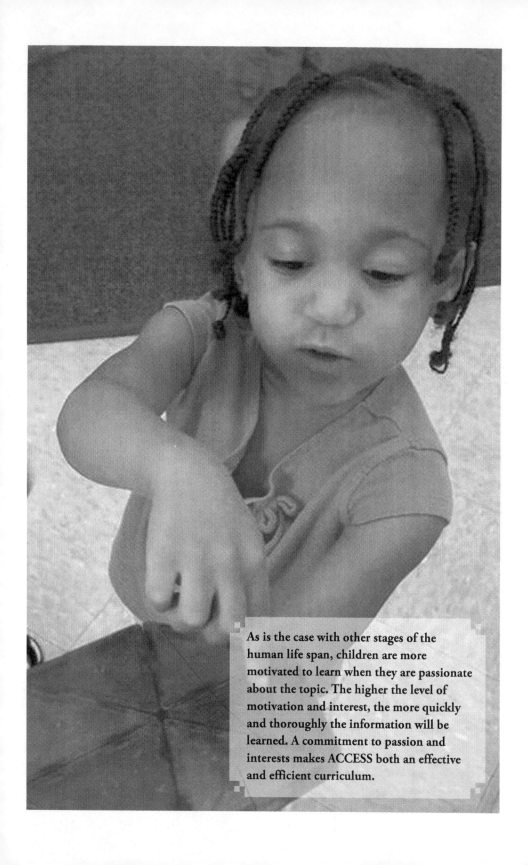

As is the case with other stages of the human life span, children are more motivated to learn when they are passionate about the topic. The higher the level of motivation and interest, the more quickly and thoroughly the information will be learned. A commitment to passion and interests makes ACCESS both an effective and efficient curriculum.

4

Emergent/Negotiated Curriculum

The wider the range of possibilities we offer children, the more intense will be their motivations and the richer their experiences. We must widen the range of topics and goals, the types of situations we offer and their degree of structure, the kinds and combinations of resources and materials, and the possible interactions with things, peers, and adults. Loris Malaguzzi, 1998, p. 79.

Engaging in extended investigations is integral to creating a curriculum that is purposeful and connected in meaningful ways. Some might believe that a child-centered curriculum means that children are the sole determiners of the topics to be studied. In reality, the teacher's lens contributes much to topic selection. *ACCESS* teachers are skilled observers of children's strengths, needs, and interests which is essential in choosing topics that are worthy of in depth study. They understand appropriate curriculum for the age of the children. They know the content they are to teach and are experts in the developmental skills that are the focus of a child-centered curriculum. Determining the topic of study is just the first step of the investigation component of *ACCESS* which is so important that it will be introduced here in Chapter 4 and will continue into the next 2 chapters. Chapter 5 will discuss the importance of extended investigations related to science topics. Finally, Chapter 6 will guide *ACCESS* teachers through the process of integrating curriculum around important topics of study.

Emergent Curriculum

ACCESS embraces the emergent curriculum model, in part, because it is the most efficient and effective method to engage children in a deep and meaningful curriculum. Human beings are more motivated to learn concepts that interest them. When we are motivated to learn, we learn more quickly and thoroughly and also commit this knowledge to long term memory which serves as the foundation to which new information is attached. In many classrooms, children spend much of their day filling time with isolated activities that do not reflect their interests. By using an emergent curriculum model, *ACCESS* teachers capitalize on the wonder and passion that young children have about the world around them.

Developmentally appropriate curriculum is both socially relevant and personally meaningful for the children in the classroom. Creating a curriculum that represents an understanding of the children, their family culture, and their region provides learning experiences that are meaningful and relevant.

Sources of Inspiration

The inspiration for the emergent curriculum and extended investigations associated with *ACCESS* comes from the Reggio Emilia Approach (Edwards, Gandini, & Forman,1993) and the Project Approach (Katz and Chard, 2000). These two approaches have inspired the field of early childhood and changed our understandings of capacity of young children.

The Reggio Emilia Approach

The Reggio Emilia Approach was developed in a small town in Italy during the post World War II reconstruction. Loris Malaguzzi established a school for young children based on the belief that they are to be empowered and provided with opportunities to construct their own knowledge as they engage in extended investigations of real world problems. He hoped to develop creative thinkers who, as adults, would have the skills to create a society void of the fascism that led to WWII. Loris Malaguzzi saw strong ties between the culture of society and how schools are formed. When reflecting on present day schooling he commiserated that, "The school and the culture separate the head from the body. They tell the child: to think without hands, to do without head, to listen and not to speak, to understand without joy, to love and to marvel only at Easter and Christmas. They tell the child: to discover the world already there and of the hundred they steal ninety-nine. They tell the child: that work and play, reality and fantasy, science and imagination, sky and earth, reason and dream, are things that do not belong together . . ." (1998, p. 5). Like many in the field of early childhood, we are inspired by the vision of Loris Malaguzzi and the teachers, parents and children of Reggio Emilia, Italy.

The Project Approach

Another inspiration for *ACCESS* is the work of Lillian Katz and Sylvia Chard who created *The Project Approach*. Katz and Chard were inspired by the Reggio Emilia Approach but realized that it did not easily translate to American culture. They shared the belief that young children are capable of deep understanding. The Project Approach includes teaching strategies to guide children through in-depth studies of real world topics and includes a complex but flexible framework that guides teachers and students through the stages of extended investigations (Katz and Chard, 2003).

113

"A project, by definition, is an in-depth investigation of a real-world topic worthy of a student's attention and effort. The study may be carried out with an entire class or with small groups of students—most often at the preschool, elementary, and middle school levels. Projects typically do not constitute the whole educational program; instead, teachers use them alongside systematic instruction and as a means of achieving curricular goals" (The Project Approach website, no date). "Projects are characterized by children asking their own questions, conducting their own investigations and making decisions about their activities" (Helm, 2001, p. 2).

The ACCESS Emergent Negotiated Curriculum

Inspired by both the Reggio Emilia and Project Approaches, *ACCESS* also sees children as capable and empowered learners. *ACCESS* is committed to an emergent but negotiated curriculum that starts with the observation of children.

The Importance of Observing Children

Before the planning process begins, teachers need to be engaged with children and adept child watchers. Embracing the notion of an emergent but negotiated curriculum, *ACCESS* teachers take copious notes about the interests of children. They stage engaging environments, bring in authentic materials, provide plenty of time for children to spend outdoors—and then, they watch. *ACCESS* teachers take anecdotal records, photographs and videos. They engage in supportive play and ask questions that inspire inquiry. They listen carefully for patterns in the questions that children ask and then they take note of the children's awe and wonderings. When a potential topic emerges, teachers add related authentic materials to the classroom and playground and point out plants, animals or phenomena in the indoor and/ or outdoor environment until they uncover the children's true level and focus of interest.

Choosing Topics that are Worthy of Study

For example, *ACCESS* teachers may see a group of children gathered around a spider on an intricate web. On the surface it may appear that the children are interested in spiders. Because the selection of a topic is an important process that can impact the curriculum for weeks or even months, an *ACCESS* teacher does not jump quickly to the decision to study spiders. Instead he or she will listen carefully to the children's wonderings as they add to the environment. Picture books about all aspects of spiders are brought into the classrooms. Authentic spider puppets are added to the dramatic play area. Yarn and tape are put on the inside of the window so that the spider's web can be recreated. Clip boards, science journals and the digital camera or tablet are made available so that children can document what they observe. The children continue to learn during this process. For the teacher, the purpose of staging the environment in this way is to uncover the aspects of the topic that interests the children the most. What started out as a study of spiders could actually become an engineering project on how spiders construct their webs.

The Context of the Curriculum

ACCESS teachers know the context of the curriculum including what children have studied in the past and what they are likely to study in the future. They archive the investigations that have taken place in their classroom with their current group of children and are also familiar with the topics studied in previous years with other teachers. "What to teach" is considered in the context of the course of study for the program across age and grade levels.

If as toddlers, the children conducted several life science investigations, then preschool teachers may choose to stage the environment to inspire the study of physical or earth science. All of these factors comprise the context which is considered in the emergent but negotiated decision-making process that determines the next topic of study.

Through ongoing interactions and observations, teachers become aware of the topics that interest the children the most. This awareness helps them identify topics that are worthy of study by this group of children.

Sources of Emergent Curriculum

- Children's interests
- Teachers' interests
- Developmental tasks
- Things in the physical environment
- People in the social environment
- Curriculum resource materials
- Serendipity—unexpected events
- Living together: conflict resolution, caregiving, and routines
- Values held in the school and community, family, and culture

(Adapted from Jones & Nimmo 1994, 127)

The Role of Technology
in an Emergent Curriculum

For many early childhood traditionalists, technology is seen as a vehicle for inappropriate practice through the use of computer based interactive workbooks. At the Bombeck Center we view technology as an important tool for research, documentation and parent communication. While the use of pre-packaged computer software for young children is deemphasized, *ACCESS* teachers in infant, toddler and preschool classrooms rely heavily on the internet to search for information using their tablets, iPads, smartphones and computers. They are careful not to allow too much information to derail an investigation. For example, if a group of children are investigating how earthworms can live in a garden without eating the fruit or vegetables, the teacher will encourage children to come up with hypotheses, conduct experiments to tests these hypotheses, and then report the results. They will not use the internet to come up with the answer to their overall research question. They may however, use technology to find out enough about earthworms to plan an experience or add to their investigation. Questions like "where do you get earthworms?", "what do they need to stay alive?" and "do they have a tail?" might be searched in the process of setting up an experiment.

Children will also use technology to record the result of the experiment. They may take a digital picture each day to see if the earthworms have eaten the apple that was placed into their habitat. They might take pictures of tadpoles as they progress through their life cycle. Capturing a picture of a block structure or a video of a play that the class acted out allows children to document projects and products that are important to them.

This young girl has discovered that if she lines the blocks up precisely and spaces them apart just right, they can knock each other over when she pushes the first one. She asked the teacher to video tape this on the iPad so that she could show her father when he picked her up that afternoon.

The Role of the Family in an Emergent Curriculum

The family is an important source of information and inspiration for possible topics of study. The teacher must understand the backgrounds and expertise of the families of the children in the room. Families are often interested in becoming involved in what is happening in the classroom and when given an idea of how they might participate, families are willing to engage in many ways. We regularly survey the families to determine how they might be interested in participating and what special areas of expertise they would be willing to share.

Family culture and home language provides input to our curriculum. The home languages of the children in the classroom determine the languages that are included in the daily routine of the class. While some programs teach Spanish as a separate class for 30 minutes to an hour a week, *ACCESS* does not advocate for pull-out second language programs. We believe that language learning should be in context, meaningful and sustained. We do not immerse children in a second language but do encourage children and families to share their home language and culture with the class.

Emergent Curriculum at Different Age Levels

Infants and Toddlers Emergent curriculum with infants and toddlers is widely accepted and considered to be preferred practice for very young children. Infant and toddler teachers follow the children's lead in order to support their rapid development across domains. As children move from infancy into toddlerhood, their attention expands and their interests become more diverse. Older infants and toddlers can show interest in a topic for investigation. For this age level the topics can spring from a favorite song or a toy that has sparked their interest. One group of older infants became fascinated in the song, "Baby Beluga" which sparked a fascination with creatures that swam in the water. Another group of toddlers became involved in their own gardening investigation after seeing what the preschoolers were growing in their garden. The investigations that toddlers complete tend to be very free-flowing and include a focus on how developmental skills can be addressed within the context of a very interesting topic of study. Science concepts tend to be foundational but opportunities for vocabulary development are abundant.

Preschoolers Emergent curriculum tends to be a very good fit for the preschool classroom. At the Bombeck Center, we group children in multiage preschool classrooms comprised of 3, 4 and 5 year olds. Investigations allow children to explore one topic at a variety of levels. The early learning and development standards for this age group tend to be very broad, and it is possible to teach most standards through a variety of investigation topics.

Kindergarten and the Primary Grades Once children enter into the primary grades, the curriculum becomes more predetermined. This doesn't mean, however, that parts of the curriculum can't be emergent. Perhaps the reading and math program requires that these subjects be taught daily through a series of sequenced lessons that addresses a hierarchy of skills. This approach may or may not be best practice, however, the district requires that the adopted reading and math programs be taught as prescribed. *ACCESS* teachers would consider those subjects to be part of the daily routine and would seek out other times of the day during which children could engage in an investigation based on interests that emerge from children. Science and social studies are common topics for investigation as the content standards tend to be broad enough to follow the children's interest. For example, an area of study in the primary grades might be focused on the life cycle which can be taught through a variety of topics. Children could study this concepts through frogs, butterflies, meal worms and even dogs or people.

Maintaining Curriculum Integrity

As content standards and accountability in the form of standardized assessment became a reality for American education, we began to notice a shift in classroom culture in our partner schools. As we observed practicum students, student teachers and interns, we witnessed a shift to a standards-based curriculum that was focused on literacy and included a series of unrelated activities. Even though teachers at the Bombeck Center were using the Project Approach, in our initial efforts to embed academic content standards into investigations, we found that the children's questions became secondary to the focus on the standards. Over time, the projects became more surface level and skill oriented and focused less on process standards. It was important to us to support investigations that delved deeply into important topics, and because of this, we opted to focus first on the questions of children. Our planning at this level did not focus on the standards because we knew that deep investigations of worthy topics would likely address the academic content standards. Instead, we allowed the children to inspire teachers, and teachers to inspire each other as they proceeded through the planning process.

Jones (2012) also noted the negative impact that resulted from standards based and standardized curriculum.

> In contrast to emergent curriculum, standardized curriculum comes from unknown experts outside the classroom. It relies on generalization rather than on an individual teacher's creativity and attentiveness to individual learners. Indeed, standardized curriculum may squelch teacher thinking. What it permits is linear planning and assessment that is responsive to bureaucratic needs in a large nation with large educational systems. In this approach, responsive teaching is sacrificed to efficiency, and only outcomes are measured (Jones, 2012, p. 67).

Jones also states that,

> Emergent curriculum focuses on the process of learning. The more standardized the curriculum, the less children's individual needs are met and the more likely it is that many children will fall behind. Children have diverse strengths. Early childhood educators, granted the flexibility to do so, can build on those strengths and on passionate interests

as they help children construct genuine knowledge for themselves and practice empathy and respect for their fellow learners. In no other way can the inhabitants of a diverse world learn to share it peaceably (2012, p 68).

Chapter Summary

Emergent curriculum is an efficient and effective method of organizing curriculum around topics of great interest. Decisions about the topics to study are made both by teacher and children who negotiate until a topic of study emerges that is highly interesting to children and also has the capability of addressing early learning and development standards. Families contribute to an emergent curriculum through their expertise and their culture. It is possible for children of all ages to participate in an emergent curriculum; however, it will look different at each age level.

ACCESS Steps to Success: Emergent Negotiated Curriculum

1. Before the year begins, become familiar with the investigations the children engaged in during the previous year. If possible talk with last year's teachers to discover areas of untapped interest.

2. Review student portfolios and other assessment data that can inform your understanding of what the children are ready to work on next.

3. Refresh your understanding of the learning and development standards for the age level of your children and review the concepts and skills that the children are likely to be working on. Keep in mind that infants and toddler tend to focus more on developmental skills, and as children become older, the amount of focus on academic content increases. Regardless of age, a challenging curriculum includes developmental skills which cannot be overlooked even with 4th and 5th graders.

4. Survey families to determine their interests, expertise and willingness to participate in the classroom.

5. Start out the year with a range of authentic materials that could inspire interest. Select materials that will attract children and encourage them to be engaged.

6. Once a topic begins to emerge, add related materials to the environment to verify the children's level of interest as well as the specific aspect of the topic that they are most interested in.

7. Continue to observe children to follow their lead to the next aspect of the investigation. Document their understandings.

References

Edwards, C. Gandini, L. & Forman, G. (Eds.) (1993). *The hundred languages of children: The Reggio Emilia approach: Advanced reflections. (2nd).* Norwood, NJ: Ablex.

Jones, E. (2012). The emergence of emergent curriculum. *Young Children* 77(3): 66-68.

Jones, E., & Nimmo, J. (1994). *Emergent curriculum.* Washington, DC: NAEYC.

Jones, E., & Reynolds, G. (2011). *The play's the thing: Teachers' roles in children's play.* (2nd) New York: Teachers College Press.

Katz, L.G. & Chard, S. (2000). *Engaging children's minds: The project approach* (2nd). Norwood, NJ: Ablex.

Malaguzzi, L. (1993). History, ideas and basic philosophy: An interview with Lella Gandini. In C. Edwards, L. Gandini & G. Forman (Eds.), *The hundred languages of children: The Reggio Emilia approach: Advanced reflections. (2nd).* Norwood, NJ: Ablex.

National Scientific Council on the Developing Child. (2011). *Building the brain's "air traffic control" system: How early experiences shape the development of executive function. http://developingchild.harvard.edu/ resources/reports_and_working_papers/*

National Scientific Council on the Developing Child. (2012). Executive function: Skills for life and learning. *In Brief. http://developingchild. harvard.edu/resources/reports_and_working_papers/*

Office of the United Nations High Commissioner for Human Rights. Convention on the Rights of the Child. General Assembly Resolution 44/25 of 20 November 1989. Available at:*www.unhchr.ch/html/menu3/b/k2crc.htm*. Accessed June 22, 2006.

Wien, C.A., (2008). *Emergent Curriculum in the Primary Classroom: Interpreting the Reggio Emilia Approach in Schools*. New York: Teachers College Press.

The teacher's role in the ACCESS curriculum is to support children as they make sense of their world in increasingly complex ways.

5

Science and Inquiry-Based

Children entering school already have substantial knowledge of the natural world, much of which is implicit . . . Contrary to older views, young children are not concrete and simplistic thinkers . . . Research shows that children's thinking is surprisingly sophisticated . . . Children can use a wide range of reasoning processes that form the underpinnings of scientific thinking, even though their experience is variable and they have much more to learn (Duschl, Schweingruber, & Shouse, 2007, pp. 2-3).

In recent times science instruction in the early years has been ignored or at best, relegated to the position of, "We'll get to it if we have time." However, recent findings suggest that the early years are indeed a fruitful and critical time for exploring the natural world in a systematic way and for developing scientific habits of mind (Eshach & Fried, 2005; Platz, 2004; Watters, Diezmann, Grieshaber, & Davis, 2000; Worth, 2010). We now know that children are able to learn more complex skills than previously thought (Saçkes, Trundle, Bell, & O'Connell, 2013). Math and science are understood to be even more essential because they are privileged domains in which "children have a natural proclivity to learn, experiment, and explore, they allow for nurturing and extending the boundaries of the learning in which children are already actively engaged. Developing and extending children's interest is particularly important in the preschool years, when attention and self-regulation are nascent abilities" (Bowman, Donovan, & Burns, 2001, pp. 8-9).

Similar to the interdependence among developmental domains described in Chapter 3, defined content subject areas overlap in the skills, knowledge and dispositions needed to successfully solve problems and engage in inquiry. Reading, writing, social studies, science and mathematics do not exist in isolation from one another as they have traditionally been taught in schools. Rather, complex thinking, understanding and problem solving in each of these content areas require the context of the others. High quality learning environments provide opportunities for children to draw upon skills in each of the developmental domains as well as each of the subject areas in order to help young children make sense of their world. Like French (2004), the *ACCESS* Curriculum is based, in part, on the notion that important science topics can be at the center of a cohesive and integrated curriculum.

The Status of Science in Today's Early Childhood Curriculum

Despite the desirability of providing young children with an integrative approach to learning and development, science is often marginalized if not completely missing from the early childhood curriculum. For many reasons, science instruction traditionally has not been a priority for teachers in preschool through third grade. For example, until recently it was believed that young children were incapable of scientific thinking and therefore it was assumed that science instruction was not developmentally appropriate. New research, however, has demonstrated that young children are quite capable of drawing from their own experiences to understand complex science concepts.

Another reason that science has been neglected in early childhood education stems from teachers' lack of confidence in their own understanding of science and their preference for other knowledge domains (Maier, Greenfield, & Bulotsky-Shearer, 2013; Hechter, 2012; Tilgner, 1990; Duschl, 1983). This research has shown that many teachers of young children lack confidence in their own science understandings and therefore are reluctant to teach science. In addition, other content areas such as reading, writing and mathematics are seen as more basic and therefore more important than science. However, with recent research highlighting the significant influence early experiences have on science learning and the advent of curriculum standards for science, many high quality early learning programs are seeking to improve science instruction for young children.

Left: This child is responding to stimuli as she tastes and maneuvers cereal in her mouth. The teacher can support science understanding by using descriptive vocabulary such as sweet, lumpy, creamy, associated with the experience. Right: This young child is moving her body through space and time. When teachers describe the movement of her body as "going down a slippery slide very fast" the child can begin to associate sensations related to physics such as gravity, friction, speed, to her physical experience.

Why Science is at the Center of the ACCESS Curriculum

Using their senses, young children are continually engaged in exploring the world around them. For example, an infant learns to recognize primary caregivers and to respond to stimuli to meet her needs. She has a favorite blanket with a soft, satin edge and shuns other rougher blankets in favor of this one. A toddler in his high chair learns that toys thrown overboard land on the ground and that peas feel different from Cheerios in his hands and mouth. A preschooler collects rocks on the playground and organizes them by color and size. A second grader is able to determine which coat to wear by reading the thermometer outside his window and examining the clouds in the sky.

In each of these cases, young children are engaged in seemingly everyday activities; however, upon closer examination the children are using exploration through trial and error to come to know and understand the properties and rules of their world. They are using their senses to observe the physical properties of people, blankets, peas, Cheerios, and rocks. They are using scientific reasoning skills to compare and contrast the properties of these objects and categorize them according to stranger/caregiver, soft/course, squishy/hard, and brown/gray/pink/white, respectively. The older child is using the tools of mathematics and number sense to read and understand the outdoor temperature and the scientific skill of making inferences to decide what coat to wear outside. In each case, the young children are expertly involved in the scientific enterprise.

Naturally occurring events like swinging provides these toddlers with an opportunity to explore foundational physics concepts. While they may not understand how momentum and gravity impact swinging, they can start to understand the cause and effects of pushing.

Young Children are Natural Scientists

Curiosity is the driving force behind childhood explorations. In no time in life is the human more authentically and openly curious than in the early childhood years. Like scientists, it is curiosity and a desire to know and understand that lead young children to explore the intricacies of the world around them. Eshach and Fried (2005) claim that young children "are already looking at the things with which science is concerned and already in the way the *best* scientists do" (p. 320, 2005).

Young children are natural scientists. Yet despite this innate curiosity and willingness to explore the world around them, little attention has been paid to science in early learning environments. Too often early learning environments do not capitalize on the curiosity of young children and fail to take advantage of the freedom that exists in quality, early learning to include rich, inquiry-based experiences (Appleton, 2007; Brenneman, Stevenson-Boyd, & Frede, 2009). For some, the neglect of science stems from a belief that young children are not at a level in their cognitive development to understand science concepts related to the world around them. For others it stems from the teachers' discomfort with science concepts and the manner in which they themselves learned science. For still others, lack of attention to science stems from the belief that pre-literacy and numeracy skills are best taught in isolation from other content.

Research suggests, however, that many of these long-held arguments for limiting science in the early learning curriculum do not hold up under scrutiny. For example, Duschl, Schweingruber, & Shouse's report for the National Research Council (2007) indicates that young children are cognitively able to develop scientific understandings of concepts related to their personal experiences. This report claims that even pre-verbal children learn a great deal about science-related concepts and can develop surprisingly sophisticated reasoning related to their own experiences with natural phenomena. Further, recent research suggests that science exploration in the early years supports learning in other domains. For example, science learning has been linked to language and literacy development (Conezio & French, 2002; Saul, 2004; Zales & Unger, 2008), the development of mathematics skills (Peterson & French, 2008) and to other cognitive developmental tasks (Anderson, Martin, & Faszewski, 2006; Ravanis & Pantidos, 2008).

Opportunities for Concept Development and Teacher-Child Interactions

Children are curious about many things around them. They play with balls, they dig in the ground, and they pick worms up off the sidewalk after the rain. All of these activities lead young children to ask question about important science topics. The possibilities are wide open for preschoolers whose "slate" is fairly blank.

The first step in designing curriculum around science is to recognize the science concepts within children's activities. Balls behave according to the laws of motion. The ground where students dig contains many plants, animals, rocks, and different types of soil. The worms on the side walk are curious creatures that only seem to surface when it rains. Each of the concepts presents interesting questions that children may wonder about. They also present a challenge to teachers who must know or be willing to learn science content well enough to guide children to the answers that they are seeking. By asking questions that lead children to important science concepts, teachers can also understand children's curiosities and conceptions of the phenomena. For example, during ball play, a teacher might ask why one ball bounces higher than another, or why one rolls faster and the other more slowly. Intentional questioning can inspire children to think and to ask more questions. The children's responses help teachers understand the children's current levels of knowledge as well as misconceptions about force and motion. To support children in their development of science concepts, teachers must first understand the concepts themselves. To this end, teacher preparation programs must require expanded coursework in science, technology, engineering and mathematics. Currently, practicing teachers need to have access to the content knowledge that supports a science focused curriculum. We recommend taking advantage of the free online professional development available at the National Science Teachers Association (NSTA) Learning Center *http://learningcenter.nsta.org*. This open access professional development is aligned with the Common Core State Standards and offers training in the areas of physical science, earth science and life science. Early childhood teachers can refresh their understanding of science concepts by taking the elementary level professional development. In addition to this professional development, it is imperative that teachers have nonfiction teaching reference books. Keep in mind that the teachers' content knowledge must be at a high enough level of understanding to support age appropriate content for the children. This does not mean that we advocate pushing down elementary level content to preschool. Teachers need deep understanding of science concepts in order to support deep but developmentally appropriate understanding in children.

These preschoolers are developing an understanding of foundational physics concepts like force, motion, and gravity as they roll balls down a tube that is serving as an inclined plane. Teachers need to have a sound understanding of these concepts in order to help children more fully understand the results of their experiment.

Studying Worthy and Age Appropriate Topics

ACCESS teachers analyze potential topics to determine which are the most worthy of study. The possibilities are wide open for preschoolers. They have their whole lives ahead of them and many years to study topics that may not be the best choice for their current age. Here are some steps that can help to make sure the topics are worthy of study and age appropriate.

Is the Topic Worthy of Study and Age Appropriate?

1. Do the children have some prior or related knowledge on which to attach these new ideas?
2. Are there opportunities for inquiry and science processes?
3. Are there opportunities to address content across other subject areas?
4. Are there opportunities to address developmental domains?
5. Is it socially relevant for children this age? For example, don't study oceans with preschoolers who live in Dayton, Ohio.
6. Is it personally meaningful for the children in the group? For example, don't study Chinese New Year unless you have a student or family member from China in the group.
7. Are there opportunities to use hands-on experiences with authentic and engaging materials? For example, the solar system is not a good topic for preschoolers as they can't touch it, taste it or smell it and there are no authentic materials to manipulate.
8. Does the child have some interest and prior knowledge on which to connect these new ideas?
9. Are there opportunities for inquiry and science processes?

Supporting Basic Science Process Skills

Basic science process skills are not unique to science. They include observing, classifying, measuring, predicting, inferring and communicating. Putting these skills to use in the service of science learning, however, is done by connecting them to other content areas and using them to explore the natural world and its properties.

As children are able to hone their powers of observation and apply the process skills to the natural world, teachers can help them develop the more advanced, integrated processes of science. These process skills include identifying and controlling variables, formulating and testing hypotheses, interpreting data, experimenting, and constructing models.

Yash's Example

The children in a preschool classroom had many questions about what happened to the food they were eating. This interest led to an investigation of the human body. The teachers collected documentation before the investigation by asking the children to draw a picture of a person. The class then completed a 4 week study which resulted in a model of a human body that included a digestive system. At the end of the investigation, the children drew another picture of a person. Notice the post investigation drawing completed by Yash after the 4 week study. It is obvious that the investigation helped Yash hone his powers of observation. Yash did not receive instructions on how to draw a person. Note how much more detailed his drawing is at the end of the investigation. His observation skills improved greatly.

Yash's first drawing included limited details and labels for the head, hair, ear, arms and legs. The body lacked hands and feet. No internal body parts were included.

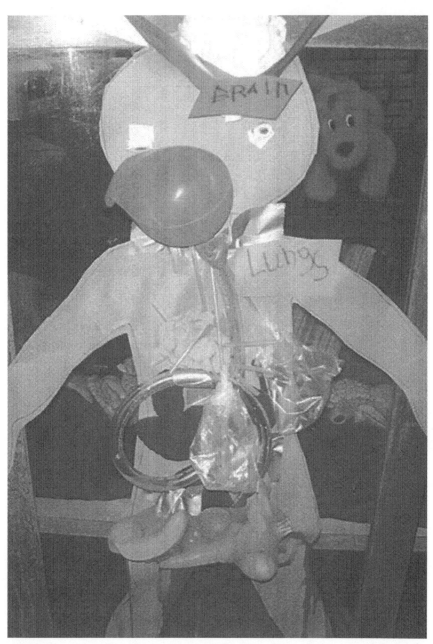

During the investigation, the children developed a model that incorporated a funnel as the mouth, with tubes representing the esophagus, intestines, and urinary track. They could pour water in and watch as it made its way through the system and into a bucket.

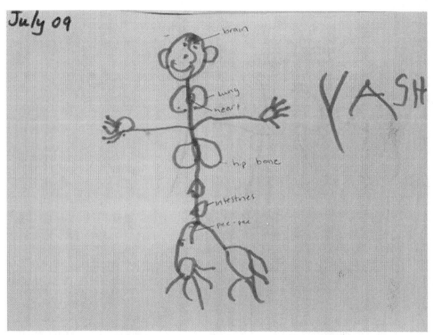

Yash's second drawing included internal body parts such as the brain, lungs, heart, hip bone, and the intestines. Although they were not addressed specifically in the investigation, Yash's observation skills were honed so well that he now included detailed hands and feet and a much more complex face. This increased attention to detail occurred over a period of 4 weeks.

To apply these concepts to children's interest in different types of balls, the investigation would look something like this:

1. Does the child have some interest?
    Yes, they brought up the subject during play and have continued to ask questions over the course of the day or a few days.

2. Are there opportunities for inquiry and science processes?
    Yes, there are several unanswered questions related to force and motion which could be answered through the science process skills. They could **observe** the bouncing patterns of different kinds of balls and develop some **predictions** of why they bounce differently. They could also roll balls down different incline surfaces and **predict** why one is faster than another. They might explore how different balls are used in different sports. They can learn to classify objects' properties by comparing and contrasting balls that are hit from those that are thrown or bounced or rolled or kicked

3. Are there opportunities to address content across other subject areas?
    Yes, math can be integrated through **measurement,** English language arts through **exploration** of children's literature, **research** into the topic, or **writing** their predictions and findings. Social studies will be included through **working together** to discover answers, **sharing** materials and **communicating** with peers and teachers in a **socially acceptable** manner. Cultures may explored by looking at the sports of different regions and the natural resources that make a particular sport popular in a particular location. The Arts can be included through **drawings**, acting out a concept through a **play** about how balls move, or developing a **song** to go with the concept.

4. Will there be opportunities to address developmental domains? Gross and fine motor skills can be addressed through the hands-on activities of the investigation. Cognition will be expanded through the learning of new concepts and application to prior learning like how balls bounce and roll. Children have the opportunity to connect real world events to a scientific concept, thus expanding their problem solving and thinking skills, plus learning new content. Communication skills include learning new vocabulary or expanding language development through conversations about the topic. Social emotional skills are naturally addressed as the children participate in shared learning.

5. Is it socially relevant and personally meaningful for children this age?
Ball play is fundamental to the development of skills related to numerous sport activities. In addition, playing with balls seems to be a universal activity of young children, making it personally meaningful.

6. Are there opportunities to use hands-on experiences with authentic and engaging materials?
Yes. Balls are 3 dimensional and easily available. There is a large variety of choices and children are easily engaged in ball play.

Other Factors to Consider

Is the topic over used? There are other factors that should be considered before choosing a science topic to use as a basis for curriculum. For example, the teacher should consider if the topic is overdone. Some topics for preschoolers, such as dinosaurs and butterflies, are studied frequently in early childhood environments. While these topics lend themselves to interesting investigations, the frequency with which they appear in curricula may indicate that new knowledge and experiences are more appropriate.

Was the topic chosen purely out of teacher interest? Another factor to consider is whether or not the topic is being skipped because of teachers' discomfort with the concepts. For example, many teachers are reluctant to teach children about physical science-related topics because of their lack of preparation. In our example with the balls, many teachers may by-pass spending time investigating forces and motion because they are uncomfortable with the concept or because they feel these concepts are not appropriate for young children. However, because of the natural curiosity and interest children have with their own play things, teachers should be willing to leave their comfort zone and pursue important topics of interest to their children.

Teachers can research the science topics and concepts related to children's interests in many ways. Libraries and curriculum materials centers are a good place to start looking for reference helpful reference materials. Many zoos, museums, aquariums, and arboretums offer professional development opportunities as well as print and electronic materials for teachers. Exploring websites of local points of interests, including parks, can yield valuable information and insight as well. In addition, local nurseries and hardware stores usually employ knowledgeable sales people who are willing to share their expertise regarding questions you might have related to their wares. For example a local garden store can provide good information on local soils and plants.

Professional organizations, such as the National Science Teachers Association (NSTA), provide many free professional development resources for teachers. NSTA provides a journal for teachers of young children (*Science & Children*) as well as workshops, seminars, print and electronic books, and blogs. Other sites also provide resources to assist teachers in developing content knowledge in specific science domains.

Websites with Science Content Resources for Teachers

National Science Teachers Association	*www.nsta.org*
Ohio Resource Center	*www.ohiorc.org*
American Association for the Advancement of Science's Science Netlinks	*www.sciencenetlinks.com*

Teachers often steer away from physical science, most likely because they have a low comfort level with physics concepts. This teacher engages these preschoolers in the study of light, reflection and mirrors.

Is the topic too abstract? A third factor to consider is whether or not the topic is too abstract for young children. Topics that are not suited to hands-on use of authentic materials should be avoided. For example, the solar system is too abstract for young children who do not have enough prior knowledge to make sense of something that they cannot see, touch or hear. Other topics are a better fit for young children, and the solar system would be a better choice for older children.

Science throughout the Classroom and the Curriculum

ACCESS adheres to the belief that science should permeate the early childhood curriculum. There should be time devoted to investigation of important science topics and other times during which children explore science more informally. Typically in preschool and primary classrooms the science center is limited to a small corner of the classroom where science tools, equipment and specimens are located. Children use this center during free play time or as part of a daily rotation of activities. However, with *ACCESS,* science should be infused throughout the classroom. In this section we will describe a well-resourced classroom for science investigation.

The Science Center

In addition to the science that is infused throughout the classroom, some *ACCESS* teachers like to stage an area of the room that is home base for the investigation. A well-stocked science center will include a variety of materials that can be used anywhere in the classroom with some items being suitable to take outdoors. In addition to consumable materials related to the investigation, other science staples that could be included in this center are:

- tools for viewing i.e. magnifiers, microscopes, specimen containers
- tools for measuring i.e. graduated cups and containers, measuring cups, measuring spoons, non-standard measurement tools, string, rulers, meter sticks, tape measures, thermometers, double pan balances, swing balance
- tools for recording observations and predictions i.e. chart paper, science journals, clip boards, notepads, pens, pencils and markers
- tools for personal and classroom safety i.e. goggles, gloves, aprons
- tools for research i.e. nonfiction/reference books, internet connected computer, tablet or IPad

Some items that could be at the science center may require more adult supervision but can add much to children's investigations. Computers, tablets/iPads and digital cameras allow children to access information as needed and also document their observations and the results of their experiments.

Living plants and animals are also often included in a science center or other area in the classroom. These elements allow children to learn to care for and observe living things. With the benefits of having living things in the classroom, comes the responsibility of knowing how to care for plants and animals and how to address any safety issues. While living things have been identified as the mark of a quality early childhood environment (Harms, Clifford and Cryer, 2005), many states have developed strict guidelines on the kinds of living things, especially animals, that can reside in the classroom. Some states ban reptiles and amphibians because of problems with bacteria. Likewise, many children are allergic to mammals which needs to be considered when choosing a classroom pet. At the Bombeck Center, every classroom has a classroom pet; however, the investigation process for choosing the pet involves researching the needs of the animal, care, cost of supplies, and state regulations by the children and teachers. In addition, the parents are asked to provide input.

Table Top Experiences

These groups of children are conducting experiments.

ACCESS teachers plan table top experiences to engage small groups of children in aspects of the investigation that require more intense scaffolding or to address the interests of individual children. Typically, table top experiences emerge from the children's questions, but it is also common for teachers to introduce new content knowledge or address misconceptions that have emerged. Another popular table top experience is conducting experiments based on the children's questions that have emerged which are related to the topic of study. Table top activities are typically conducted as one option during free choice time. By observing children throughout other parts of the day, teachers can determine the kinds of activities to be planned for a table top experience.

The Block Area

Another important area of the room that supports science, math and engineering concepts is the block area. In this area children experiment with force and motion as they make ramps. They are using principles of architecture and engineering as they build structures and begin to understand gravity, sorting, geometry and the planning process. As they learn to stack, they come to understand the effects of gravity as well as the importance of balance and symmetry. Ramps and vehicles can be added as children progress in their work with blocks. Wide, flat blocks can be used to form ramps with smaller blocks being used to change the ramp height. When rolling vehicles are added, children have opportunities to investigate force and motion and the effects of incline planes on speed and distance travelled. Older children would benefit from having non-standard and standard measuring tools available in this area so that they can learn to collect data about distances and the relationships to ramp height. The teacher can help children to recognize the science that is happening by using the language of science to label children's ideas and actions and to ask questions that help children recognize and use science process skills.

Water Play

Water tables are an excellent place to explore science concepts. By providing appropriate resources/materials in the water table area, children will be able to explore density, properties of a liquid and measurement. For example, with a variety of objects of different sizes, shapes, and composition, children will be able to explore the properties of density through testing and observing which things sink and which things float and how they are similar and different. By providing labeled measuring cups rather than non-labeled containers, children will begin to investigate how liquids pour and are measured, and begin to explore proportional reasoning. Older children can begin to investigate surface tension when given eye droppers and small coins or paper clips.

The Dramatic Play Area

The dramatic play area serves as an excellent place for children to practice the skills of science as well as imagine their own role as scientist. Materials in this area might include the tools of science, just as they include the tools of kitchens and households. In the dramatic play area children can sort foods, examine textures of the different types of clothes or cloths and even play scientist. Toy magnifiers, microscopes, animal replicas, bug boxes, safety goggles, lab coats and so forth add materials for creative play and role exploration. The inclusion of realistic puppets can also serve as a creative prop for children's imaginations. Sorting and classifying are two important science processes. Even storing materials in different types of containers, woven baskets, wooden bowls, clear and opaque plastic can give children opportunities to examine and compare materials as well as improve their spatial skills.

Manipulatives

Manipulatives provide children an opportunity to create and examine the properties of different materials, teachers select from a wide range of materials that can support investigations or foundational concepts like shape. It is common for the manipulative center to have materials that support visual spatial development. Puzzles, geo shapes, Legos, nonstandard measuring tools, and sorting objects are common materials in this center. Some classrooms augment this center with a light table. In considering what materials to put in this area, teachers should imagine that children are asking the following questions as they work with the materials. What will these materials do? How can I combine the materials to create something new? What can I do with this magnet? As children interact with the materials in this area, they are provided with opportunities for creative problem solving and complex thinking.

The Art Center

The art center is an ideal place for young children to hone their observation and communication skills. Through careful, systematic observation children learn to pay attention to details. As they describe their new understandings through drawing, painting, and model building they begin to refine their observation skills, seeking, for example, to more accurately represent the structure of an insect or to test their ideas about how pitch is affected by shape and material. In order to recreate an insect, children must make close observations of a real insect, noting the number and placement of body parts. Likewise, children can examine how form impacts function. For example, if the legs of the insect are placed too close together, the insect will not be able to stand. In another example, the children in the picture on the right wanted to recreate a musical instrument. After visually observing the structure of the instrument and listening to the sounds it made they wanted to recreate the vibration of the strings. In order to do this they experimented with different shapes and materials to create a box guitar.

Sand Play

Sand is one of the basic materials of Earth. Through sand play, children discover how water can change the appearance and properties of sand. Wet sand will pack, dry sand pours like a liquid but it is a solid. Sand can be measured, has weight, texture and depending on the type of sand, different colors. Teachers need to be aware of the safety issues related to sand. Sand that is identified for use with children is imperative as other types of sand can be harmful. Sand that is used outdoors needs to be covered when not in use as it can be soiled by animals.

The Reading Center

Nonfiction books are underrepresented in early childhood classrooms. Intentionally selecting both fiction and nonfiction books on science topics supports both inquiry and literacy.

Selecting high quality books for teaching science to young children can be challenging. While each year a plethora of books related to science topics and phenomena are published, teachers need to be vigilant in selecting those that are most appropriate for the particular children and their interests as well as those that are scientifically accurate. Buxton and Austin (2003) present five considerations for selecting science trade books for children. First they suggest that high quality books show science as connecting to children's everyday lives. These books demonstrate that science is everywhere and part of everything we do. Second, Buxton and Austin suggest high quality books are engaging and present science through enjoyable, memorable stories. Third, they propose that high quality science books for children show how the "expert" scientists use the specific inquiry skills that they are also using. This demonstrates to children that the skills they are using to investigate the world around them are valid and reliable and are the same as those used by the experts. To combat the negative, detached stereotype of science and scientists that is present in the culture at large, Buxton and Austin suggest that high quality books for children personalize and humanize science, showing how scientists are real people with a passion for what they do. Finally, Buxton and Austin recommend that high quality books about science for children highlight the developmental nature of science. Science is not stagnant and scientific "facts" are continually revised over time as new information is discovered. A view of the nature of science helps children to understand their place in the advancement of science rather leading them to believe that there are no more questions to be answered.

While Buxton and Austin's (2003) suggestions provide a framework for selecting books that are compatible with the nature of science, Rice, Dudley, and Williams (2001) provide a series of questions that a teacher should ask when choosing children's literature to teach science that focuses more on the scientific accuracy of the text and illustrations. This list of questions that follow should help a teacher select high quality, scientifically accurate texts.

Checklist for Choosing Children's Literature to Teach Science

- Is the science concept recognizable?
- Is the story factual?
- Is fact discernible from fiction?
- Does the book contain misrepresentations?
- Are the illustrations accurate?
- Are characters portrayed with gender equity?
- Are animals portrayed naturally?
- Is the passage of time referenced adequately?
- Does the story promote a positive attitude toward science and technology?
- Will children read or listen to this book?

(Rice, Dudley, & Williams, 2001, p. 21)

While these tips and checklists can help teachers to assess the quality of books, finding high quality books can be a challenge. Local libraries have multiple resources that teachers can use in their classrooms. A local children's literature librarian can be an invaluable resource in locating appropriate books. Note that the teacher will still need to use the guidelines here in choosing which books are most appropriate and useful for his or her children. The websites below offer a place to locate high quality books for children.

Websites with Recommendations for High Quality Science Books for Children

National Science Teachers Association, *Science and Children* (Each issue includes a feature called *Teaching with Trade Books* that gives recommendations for books and lessons)

http://www.nsta.org/publications/search_journals. aspx?keyword=Teaching%20with%20Trade%20Books&journal=SC

National Science Teachers Association, Outstanding Science Trade Books for Students (Published annually, this list of new trade books is peer reviewed)

http://www.nsta.org/publications/ostb/

Ohio Resource Center, Science Bookshelf

http://www.ohiorc.org/bookshelf/

Circle Time

Circle time is an opportunity for the teacher to read books and share information but is also a time for children and teachers to discuss and talk about science. Science talks involve teachers and children listening to each other's ideas and theories about how the world works. Using circle time to create classroom charts record children's ideas and comments can turn a onetime circle experience into an ongoing learning experience.

The Music Center

Music is important in the early childhood curriculum in general. In the science curriculum, music can be part of a study of sound or a means of helping children remember other science concepts. *ACCESS* teachers use a collection of songs written and performed by Julianne Lasley Garrison. The series of 23 science songs were developed to provide children with a musical way to learn and remember science concepts. Children enjoy these songs because of the variety of genre and unique topics. Many songs incorporate movement as well. The songs are available to be downloaded as part of the *ACCESS* collection at *www.accesscurriculum.com* which includes the following titles:

1. Bud's Bridge
2. Beaks and Feet
3. Like a Scientist
4. Our Bodies
5. Mixing
6. Living Things
7. Mammals
8. Rock Walk
9. Magnets
10. Gravity
11. Levers, Wedges, and Screws
12. Seeds and Plants
13. Our Hands
14. Spinning
15. Spin Fast, Spin Slow
16. A Star!
17. Night Stars!
18. Rolling
19. Textures
20. Marching
21. Bouncing
22. Twinkle Twinkle Little Star
23. Five Senses!

Science Outside

Physics on the Playground

Force and motion and the different ways we can make things move is only the tip of the ice berg on what can be discovered in the outdoors. In even the most urban of play areas, the natural world can be discovered: ants crawling, grass growing in the cracks of the asphalt, birds and squirrels or other small creatures may be discovered. The key to making the most of the outdoor environment is the teacher scaffolding the children, identifying or labeling what is happening, using the language of science to help children connect their exploration and play to science concepts.

Weather

The study of weather is inexpensive, authentic and multi-sensory.

When thinking about how science is taught, it is important to push past our current traditions. For example, it is common in many preschool and primary classrooms to start out the day with a morning meeting that includes the calendar and charting weather conditions using a cartoon sunshine poster. While a commonly accepted practice, is this really the best way to teach weather? Should weather, the quintessential multi-sensory experience, be relegated to a 2 dimensional labeling activity? *ACCESS* asks teachers to take advantage of authentic science experiences, and weather is one of the best and cheapest authentic experience, readily available, observable, and recordable. The concept of weather is complex and can be studied on many different levels. It can support academic content in science, language arts, math, social studies and the arts. It can also provide experiences related to developmental skills across all domains.

Consider this example with Mr. Eric who turned his first graders' walk from breakfast to their classroom into a yearlong weather exploration. By placing some inexpensive weather instruments at the children's level in the breezeway that the class walked through every morning and afternoon, Mr. Eric created a weather observatory. He provided clipboards upon which they could record data and assigned roles so that all children were involved in the investigation over the course of a week. The children started out by following Eric's lead as they read the gauges and made simple observations based on his directions. After a while the children made up their own weather experiments like filling the concrete handprint with water to see how quickly the water evaporated, froze or thawed.

By the end of September, they decided to take a picture of a deciduous tree each Monday to see how weather and the season changed the tree. By Christmas, the first graders were emailing their weather reports to the local news. Mr. Eric noted that the five to ten minutes a day spent on weather observations fostered inquiry and used time that was otherwise wasted. He also noted that his students had a much more comprehensive understanding of seasons than other children who used a holiday approach. His children experienced the length of time that the seasons took to transition because they focused intensely to changes in their environment. One very meaningful strategy in this study was taking the weekly photo of the same tree. They inserted the photo into an ongoing PowerPoint slideshow which they watched repeatedly through the year. The slow changes that they captured overtime became clear documentation of the change of seasons which unfolded before them.

Photo by Ivan Kmit. 123RF

Gardening

Gardening is an annual occurrence and important part of the school's culture. Starting in February children discuss and plan their garden. They taste vegetables and vote to determine the favorites. They negotiate how much garden space to devote to each vegetable and decide whether or not to plant flowers. They plant seeds and cultivate seedlings while discussing what plants need to grow. As the weather warms, the children explore their garden options considering the garden plots, raised beds and containers. They decide what to plant where and when to begin planting. They spend the summer weeding and watering while they watch for helpful and harmful insects. The role of worms in the soil is a frequent area of interest. As vegetables are ready for harvest, the farmers market is opened for parents during drop off and pick up times. With the market comes marketing and economics which can take the investigation in a different directly.

Consider an investigation of insects, worms or spiders.

Trees, erosion, and pond scum can be teachable moments that are worthy of study.

Setting up a Science Focused Classroom

Teachers and administrators have come to rely on environment rating skills as part of an annual self-study designed for continuous improvement. These tools are research-based and are highly regarded in the field when working with infants, toddlers and preschoolers. For teachers who wish to emphasize science and inquiry as the center of the curriculum, more science needs to be evident throughout the classroom. To support teachers who want a structure for setting up a science focused classroom, we have created a tool entitled the *Early Childhood Science/Nature Environment Rating Scale* (ECSERS) (see figure 5-1). This tool mirrors the format of such popular tools as the *Early Childhood Environment Rating Scale* (Harms, Clifford & Cryer, 2009) and can be used in conjunction with other environment rating scales. The ECSERS is designed for use in preschool and primary grades classrooms and provides detailed criteria for setting up a classroom that is well equipped to focus on science.

155

Figure 5-1 Early Childhood Science/Nature Environment Rating Scale

Location_____Teacher_____

Early Childhood Science/Nature Environment Rating Scale

Inadequate		Minimal	
1	**2**	**3**	**4**

Science /Nature (expanded)

1.1 No science tools accessible to students.	3.1 Some science tools accessible, but only through an adult.
1.2 No science safety equipment present.	3.2 Science safety equipment present, but unused.
1.3. No natural science materials are present.	3.3 Some natural science materials are available.
1.4 No displays of children's science thinking.	3.4 Children's science thinking is referred to but is not displayed.
1.5 No science reference materials are available.	3.5 Some science reference materials available to children.
1.6 No science materials evident and available in the classroom.	3.6 Science materials evident in one area of the classroom.
1.7 No outdoor science environments are available to children.	3.7 One or two outdoor science environments are occasionally available for exploration.

NOTES

.0 Elements.1 through .6 refer specifically to indoor spaces

.1 Readily available placement of DAP science tools (i.e., magnifiers, prisms, magnets, mirrors, flashlights, pan balances, measuring cups and spoons, bug boxes, etc.

.2 DAP science safety equipment (i.e .eye protection, smocks, gloves, etc.)

.3 A variety of natural materials are displayed and available (i.e., predictions, graphs, charts, before and after activity work samples, etc.

_____Date_____Evaluator_____

Good		Excellent
5	**6**	**7**

5.1 Many science tools accessible to children.

7.1 Science tools used on a frequent basis by children in free play and/or in structured activities.

5.2 Science safety equipment is openly accessible to children but used only when prompted by adult.

7.2 Science safety equipment used on a regular basis by children in free play or in structured activities.

5.3 A wide variety of natural science materials are displayed and available for children's use.

7.3 Children regularly use and engage with natural science materials.

5.4 Some examples of children's science thinking is displayed.

7.4 Children's science thinking is prominently displayed and children can describe their display.

5.5 A variety of science reference materials reflecting one or two science areas (topics) is openly displayed and available to children.

7.5 A wide variety (3 or more topics) of science reference materials is openly displayed and available to children.

5.6 Science materials evident and available in two areas of the classroom.

7.6 Science materials evident and available in multiple areas of the classroom.

5.7 One or two outdoor science environment are available for exploration by children and is used on a regular basis.

7.7 A variety of outdoor science environments is open to exploration by children on a daily basis for free play and/or structured activities.

NOTES

.4 Displays of children's science thinking are prominent (i.e., predictions, graphs, charts, before and after activity work samples, etc.

.5 Variety of relevant science reference materials are openly available (i.e., children's field guides, posters, non-fiction books, etc.).

.6 No explanatory comments.

.7 Outdoor science environments are available to children on a regular basis.

The format of this scale was inspired by the Environmental Rating Scales developed by Harms, Clifford, and Cryer

Chapter Summary

This chapter provided extensive explanation for why science should be the center of the early childhood curriculum. While young children are well suited for extensive study of science, many early childhood teachers are reticent to fully engage in science instruction. Whether because of a lack of confidence in their own science content knowledge or a preference to teach other subject areas, many early childhood teachers do not teach science. To address this problem, examples of how to set up an environment that supports science learning throughout the classroom and playground were provided. Finally, a tool for self-assessment was provided to help teachers stage an environment that fully supports science instruction.

ACCESS Steps to Success: Science and Inquiry

1. Observe children's knowledge, experiences, and interests when selecting a topic for investigation.
2. Select a science topic for investigation that provides opportunities for use of inquiry and the science processes, naturally integrates other content areas and developmental domains, is personally meaningful and socially relevant for children, and provides opportunities to interact with authentic, engaging materials.
3. Develop your own science content knowledge pertinent to the topic you have selected by engaging in professional development through workshops, blogs, and research.
4. Use the science concept planner to design experiences for your children that will allow them to investigate the topic.
5. Gather developmentally appropriate, multisensory, authentic materials that can be utilized throughout your classroom and outdoor environment to stimulate children's interest, questioning, and problem solving related to the topic.
6. Gather high quality, developmentally appropriate, engaging print materials, including fiction and non-fiction books which children will find interesting and useful either on their own or with adult support.
7. Allow time in your classroom for the topic to evolve. Guide student questions, experiences, interests, and investigations into relevant questions by providing multiple experiences to investigate the topic.

References

Anderson, K. L., Martin, D. M., & Faszewski, E. E. (2006). Unlocking the power of observations. *Science & Children, 44*(1), 32-35.

Appleton, K. 2007. Elementary science teaching. In S. K. Abell & N. G. Ledermann (eds.), *Handbook of research on science education*. Mahwah, NJ: Lawrence Erlbaum, 493-535.

Baldwin, J.L., Adams, S.M., Comingore, J.L. & Kelly, M.K. (2009). Science at the center: An emergent, standards-based, child-centered framework for early learners. *Early Childhood Education, 37*(1), 71-77.

Bowman, B. T., Donovan, M. S., & Burns, M. S. (Eds.). (2001). *Eager to learn: Educating our preschoolers*. Washington, DC: National Academy Press.

Brenneman, K., Stevenson-Boyd, J., & Frede, E. C. (2009). Math and science in preschool: Policies and practices. *National Institute for Early Education Research Preschool Policy Brief, 19*.

Buxton, C. A. & Austin, P. (2003) Better books better teaching. *Science & Children, 41*(2), 28-32.

Conezio, K., & French, L. (2002). Science in the preschool classroom: Capitalizing on children's fascination with the everyday world to foster language and literacy development. *Young Children, 57*(5), 12-18. Retrieved from *www.journal.naeyc.org/btj/200209*.

Duschl, R. A., Schweingruber, H. A. & Shouse, A. W. (Eds.) (2007). *Taking science to school: Learning and teaching science in grades K-8*. Washington, DC: National Academies Press.

Eidietis, L, Jewkes, A. M. (2011). Making curriculum decisions in K-8 science: The relationship between teacher dispositions and curriculum content. *Journal of Geoscience Education*, (59), 4, 242.

Eshach, H., & Fried M. N. (2005). Should science be taught in early childhood? *Journal of Science Education and Technology*, 14(3), 315-336.

French, L. (2004). Science as the center of a coherent, integrated early childhood curriculum. *Early Childhood Research Quarterly*, 19(1), 138.

Hechter, R. P. (2011). Changes in Preservice Elementary Teachers' Personal Science Teaching Efficacy and Science Teaching Outcome Expectancies: The Influence of Context. *Journal of Science Teacher Education* (22) 2, p. 187.

Maier, M.F., Greenfield, D.B., & Bulotsky-Shearer, R.J. (2013) Development and validation of a preschool teachers' attitudes and beliefs toward science teaching questionnaire. *Early Childhood Research Quarterly*, 28 (2), 366.

Peterson, S. M., & French, L. (2008). Supporting young children's explanations through inquiry science in preschool. *Early Childhood Research Quarterly, 23*(3), 395-408.

Platz, D. L. (2004). Challenging young children through simple sorting and classifying: a developmental approach. *Education*, 125(1), 88-96.

Ravanis, K., & Pantidos, P. (2008). Sciences activities in preschool education: Effective and ineffective activities in a Piagetian theoretical framework for research and development. *International Journal of Learning, 15*(2), 123-132.

Saçkes, M., Trundle, K.C., Bell, R. L., & O'Connell, A. A. (2011), The influence of early science experience in kindergarten on children's immediate and later science achievement: Evidence from the early childhood longitudinal study. *Journal of Research in Science Teaching*, 48, (2).

Saul, E. W. (Ed.). (2004). *Crossing borders in literacy and science instruction: Perspectives on theory and practice.* Newark, DE, International Reading Association.

Tilgner, P.J. (1990), Avoiding science in the elementary school. *Science Education*, 74 (4) 421-431.

Watters, J. J., Diezmann, C. M., Grieshaber, S. J., & Davis, J. M. (2000). Enhancing science education for young children: A contemporary initiative. *Australian Journal of Early Childhood*, 26 (2).

Worth, K. (2010). Science in Early Childhood Classrooms: Content and Process. *Early Childhood Research and Practice: SEED Papers* (fall).

Zales, C. R., & Unger, C. S. (2008). The science and literacy framework. *Science & Children, 46*(3), 42-44.

An investigation into musical instruments provides a wonderful opportunity to integrate content standards in language arts, social studies, mathematics and science, through a study of sound, while also working on developmental skills such as imitation, sharing, communication and fine motor control.

6

Standards Integrated

The Association for Supervision and Curriculum Development (ASCD) states that a "good curriculum" provides opportunities for students and teachers to study important topics and skills in depth versus the inch deep and mile wide curriculum that is common in classrooms today (2004).

A common criticism of today's American educational system is that children are taught through a series of unrelated activities resulting in a broad curriculum that has little depth. For example, the U.S. mathematics curriculum has been characterized as broad but superficial and fragmented rather than coherent (Newton, 2007). In part to address this issue, the Common Core State Standards (CCSS) (National Governors Association Center for Best Practices & Council of Chief State School Officers, 2010) include a strong emphasis on integrating curriculum. Currently 45 states now use the CCSS for curriculum planning (Garelick, 2012), and the impact on instruction in grades kindergarten through 12 is substantial. Preschool curriculum is also impacted because many states have aligned early learning content and development standards with the CCSS.

The Association for Supervision and Curriculum Development (ASCD) states that a "good curriculum" provides opportunities for students and teachers to study important topics and skills in depth versus the inch deep and mile wide curriculum that is common in classrooms today (2004). A recent consensus statement developed by ASCD and other educational organizations have lobbied for funding for all discipline specific subjects as "the interrelationship among disciplines enhances learning and understanding for each student." In addition, grant money is being recommended to "emphasize best practices, scalability, and cross-subject collaboration and integration" (Retrieved, 4/27/2013).

Common Practices K-Primary

With the call for integrated curriculum, why do we still have fragmented curriculum practices in the classroom? One way to consider this question is to examine how curriculum and instruction are constructed at the classroom level where it is common for teachers to plan in isolation and to rely heavily on teacher resources such as curriculum guides and teachers' manuals. In many cases kindergarten and primary grades teachers do not use assessment data in the planning process, and many teachers plan for two purposes: 1) to teach the content defined by CCSS and/or, as appropriate, the course of study; and 2) to meet the required time allotted to each subject area. In many classrooms children fill their day traveling from one discrete lesson to the next, and because the lessons are not required to be connected, children often complete their education without the benefit of a coherent curriculum.

Planning in Early Childhood Programs

This lack of connection between experiences is common with older children, but does it also apply to programs serving younger children? Consider the following preschool schedule that is typical for many early childhood programs.

TYPICAL PRESCHOOL DAILY ROUTINE

ARRIVAL and WELCOME
MORNING MEETING: Weather, Calendar and Job Chart,
    Planning Time
FREE CHOICE: Housekeeping, Dramatic Play, Blocks,
    Manipulatives, Science/Nature, Center, Sand and Water Table,
    Art, Reading Area, Computer
CIRCLE TIME: Story Book Reading, Songs and Finger Plays
SNACK: often laid out by staff with minimal child learning evident
LEARNING CENTERS: Writing Centers, Number Concepts, Arts
    and Crafts
OUTDOOR PLAY: Slide/Swing, Sandbox, Riding Toys
WRAP UP AND GET READY TO GO HOME

Without a unifying topic, it is likely that this preschool day will be filled with a series of disconnected activities and that the early childhood curriculum will lack cohesiveness.

Looking at a common 1st grade schedule continues the practice of isolated skill development. Cohesiveness is not a concern for the teacher who has planned this day where addressing content standards and isolated instruction is the norm.

Typical 1st Grade Schedule/Routine

- 8:00-8:30   Arrival, Morning Work and Play
- 8:30-10:55   Reading Block
- 10:15   Snack
- 11:00-12:40   Lunch, Recess and Specials
- 12:50-1:50   Math
- 1:50-2:25   Writer's Workshop
- 2:25-2:45   Clean up classroom, Prepare to go home
- 2:45   Dismissal

Intentional Planning with ACCESS

Teachers using *ACCESS* are intentional about establishing daily routines and planning extended investigations that integrate content standards across all disciplines and development across all domains.

The Importance of Daily Routine in the Infant/Toddler Classroom

Teachers using *ACCESS* in infant and toddler classrooms describe the daily routine as an important vehicle for unifying the experiences of the children in the classroom. Because the job of infants and toddlers is to make sense of their world, their curriculum reflects authentic and naturally occurring events within the classroom routine. *ACCESS* for infants and toddlers is "routine-based" and relies on teachers who are intentional in looking for opportunities to support development across all domains. To this end, Bombeck Center infant and toddler teachers have created a series of documents that show clearly how a routine such as hand washing helps children understand the sequence of the day and therefore be able to anticipate what will come next. These charts show how daily routines provide learning experiences across all developmental domains for infants and toddlers (See Figure 6-1).

The handwashing routine is an important teachable moment for infants and toddlers.

Figure 6-1: Bombeck Family Learning Center-Infant/Toddler Daily Experiences

Physical Health	Emotional Development	Social Development
Health Care Universal health precautions are followed to eliminate germs	**Attachment** Child will form strong bonds with caregiver who assists them during hand washing	**Attachment** The bond between the caregiver and child strengthens as adult assists the child in hand washing process
Hand Washing Caregivers and child will follow proper hand washing techniques. Children and adults wash their hands before and after meals, after sensory and outdoor play, upon entering and leaving the center and whenever hands become soiled	**Expression of Emotion** Child will laugh and smile, looking at self in the mirror while experiencing soap and water **Self-Awareness** Child will begin to differentiate parts of his/her hands and arms	**Interaction with Adults** Caregivers will make the hand washing process enjoyable (i.e. singing to time washing hands)
Diapering and Toileting Children are taught the proper hand washing procedures. Caregivers model washing hands after changing diapers or assisting with toileting and assist child in washing their hands as well	**Awareness of Emotion** Caregivers will support the child as he/she becomes aware of dealing with the frustration of taking turns during hand washing	**Interaction with Peers** Child will be supported as he/she interacts with peers when waiting for a turn
	Sense of Competence Child will develop confidence in his/her ability to wash hands, use soap dispenser and get his/her own towel	**Empathy** Child will be encouraged to assist peers with paper towel or soap
	Self-Comforting Child will use sensory experience of warm water, soft foamy soap to self-comfort	**Social Identity** Child will participate in the process doing as much as possible independently
	Impulse Control Child learns appropriate response to others as he/she waits to take turns and to accept termination of hand washing	

Motor Development	Language Development	Cognitive Development
Movement/Balance and Coordination Child will be supported as he/she stands on the platform to reach sink and remain upright while washing hands	**Understanding Language** Child will understand and follow simple hand washing directions. Caregivers will describe the process as they assist the child	**Group and Categorize** Child will place paper products in the proper container
		Cause and Effect Child sees how he/she affects the flow of water by turning faucets on and off
Touch/Grasp/Reach and Manipulate Child will turn on the faucet, pump, the soap dispenser, push handle of towel dispenser with assistance as needed	**Expressing Language** Child will be encouraged to indicate if he/she needs to wash hands or needs help in the process	**Problem Solving** Child is supported as he/she figures out how to push the lever to dispense soap, pull lever to dispense towel, and tear off towel
Oral motor Child will talk to self and make faces moving mouth as he/she looks in the mirror during hand washing	**Rules of Language** Child carries on conversations with caregivers and peers while in the bath room or at sinks	**Memory** Child will demonstrate an understanding of the proper procedures and appropriate times to wash hands
	Early Literacy Printed signs and numbers are posted in the bathroom. Caregivers point out the "h" for hot and the "c" for cold on the faucets	**Space** Caregiver will support child as he/she learns to operate soap/towel dispenser/faucet and step on and off the platform
	Early Writing The hand washing process helps develop muscle tone needed for writing/mark making	**Attention and Persistence** Child will wash for longer period of time (min. 10 sec.) with support as needed
		Imitation Child will watch others wash hands and do the same

The full collection of charts for daily experiences is available in the *ACCESS* Collection at *www.accesscurriculum.com* and includes intentional analyses of the following key infant and toddler routines:

1. Meeting
2. Meals/Bottles
3. Diapering/Toileting
4. Hand Washing
5. Nap
6. Motor Skills (Large/Small-Gym, Outdoors, Art, Pre-writing, Classroom)
7. Play/Learning Experiences (Intentional & Child-Centered)

Themes, Units, Projects and Investigations

What strategies have been tried to bring continuity to infant, toddler, preschool and primary grades classrooms?

Themes and Units

It is common for early childhood teachers to attempt to make connections between activities by implementing a series of themes or units. Many teachers plan these themes or units well in advance, sometimes before the school year begins. Many themes are based on seasons and holidays, but few relate to the interests, strengths, needs or family cultures of the children in the classroom. Frequently, early childhood classrooms start the year with a "friends" theme and move on to "apples" in September, "leaves, pumpkins or Halloween" in October, followed by "Thanksgiving" in November and "winter" and/ or "Christmas" in December. Themes are often based on surface level connections that loosely tie activities, events and room decorations together. Themes typically do not include an in-depth study or opportunities for children to engage in inquiry.

One example of how a superficial theme versus an in-depth study is planned is the common November theme of Thanksgiving. A visit to many preschool and primary grades classrooms in November will result in an opportunity to watch children make hand-shaped, paper turkeys. The study of Thanksgiving is often relegated to children dressing up in decorated grocery sack vests and construction paper headdresses, perpetuating a Native American stereotype and adding little depth to the children's understanding of this American tradition.

In contrast, a more in-depth approach for primary classrooms might include an authentic study of Native American's who live or lived in the geographic region in which the children reside. The students could also explore what life was like during the time of the Pilgrims or engage in a more factual study of what actually occurred during the first Thanksgiving. For preschool-aged children, a more in-depth and appropriate study might be "the harvest" including the many types and uses for the fruits and vegetables that are harvested in the fall. If the child's family recognizes and celebrates Thanksgiving, he/she could share his/her social traditions, compare those traditions to that of his/her peers and discover the place of celebrations in the culture of a society.

Another mainstay is the common theme of "teddy bears." The internet is filled with ideas for teachers to carry out this theme with bear shaped worksheets, bulletin board dressings and recipes for Teddy Bear Picnics. This theme is perpetuated by "readily available" and "cute" teacher materials which end up with "fun" activities for children; however, is "cute," "fun" and "readily available" enough of a reason to intentionally teach this theme? Are teachers who choose these themes reflecting on the strengths, needs and interests of their students in order to select topics of study that are intellectually challenging? Katz and Chard (1998) argue for more substantial and extended studies of worthwhile topics that they call "projects." They state that:

> Teachers have the ultimate responsibility for selecting the topics for projects undertaken by their pupils. But the number of possible topics for projects is so large that it is a good idea to have some bases for deciding which are appropriate to the children's intellectual development. The best project topics are those that enable children to strengthen their natural dispositions to be interested, absorbed, and involved in in-depth observation and investigation, and to represent that learning in a wide variety of ways in their classrooms (p 5).

This would suggest that "themes" or "units" may not be the best strategy to unify curriculum as children need to be interested, absorbed, and involved in in-depth observation and investigation. Katz and Chard would suggest that there are topics that are more worthy of study and developmentally appropriate than teddy bears and the stereotyped Thanksgiving lessons so common in American classrooms (1998). Katz and Chard also note that, "Unlike units and themes in the early childhood and primary curriculum, projects are defined as children's in-depth investigations of various topics— ideally, topics worthy of the children's time and energy" (1998, p 1).

171

ACCESS: Integrating Curriculum around Important Science Topics of Study

As mentioned in earlier chapters, *ACCESS* provides the tools for teachers to utilize assessment data as well as the *Science Concept Planner* to make instructional decisions. By starting at the center of the planner with an important science topic and using accurate content information to identify key concepts to be addressed, teachers are able to design instruction that is coherent, connected and meaningful. Instead of themes or units, *ACCESS* relies on big ideas that lead to enduring understanding of important science topics. As described in chapter 5, instructional decisions start with the science topic, then to accurate science concepts and then to relevant experiences that teach those concepts.

To begin, consider the *Science Concept Planner* in figure 6-2. In this example, teachers completed a brainstorming session in which they identified 4 key concepts related to their science topic, bridges. They then identified experiences that would support children in understanding the concepts. The teachers had conversations with children and engaged in focused observations in order to identify the questions and misconceptions that emerged about the topic. The teachers worked hard to focus on the concepts first before identifying experiences. They avoided moving too quickly to "activities" which are chosen because they are "cute," "fun" and "readily available." Instead, they chose activities that supported inquiry or the understanding of the concepts related to the topic of investigation.

Construction can be a topic that is worthy of study and it addressing the engineering component of a STEM curriculum.

Figure 6-2: Science Concept Planner—Bridges

Experience: Compare wood, stone, iron (steel)
Standards: Explores objects, materials and events in the environment
Makes inferences, generalizations and explanations based on evidence
Developmental Domain/s: cognitive, motor

Experience: Explore arches
Standards: Determines meaning of words
Identifies/describes/creates shapes
Developmental Domain/s: motor, cognitive

*Experience: Draw plans for beam bridges including the deck, abutments and piers
Standards: Uses drawings and visuals to support language
Developmental Domain/s: fine motor and language

*Experience: Suspension: towers, cables, anchors and hangers
Standards: Shares findings, ideas and explanations through variety of methods
Uses creative and flexible thinking to solve problems
Developmental Domain/s: cognitive, motor, social

*potential learning/teaching experiences

Concept: 1
Types of bridges:
Arch
Beam
Suspension

Reference materials are used to identify/inform the topic.

Experience: Make concrete
Standards: Uses classroom & household tools independently to carry out activities, follows simple directions
Developmental Domain/s: cognitive, motor

Concept: 4
Materials used to construct bridges
wood, stone, iron

Topic:
Bridges

Experience*
Introduce Compression: push or squeeze
Sponge & water
Pile it on. Smashing marshmallows
Standards:
Demonstrates loco-motor skills, coordination, spatial awareness
Identifies less/more
Developmental Domain/s: motor, cognitive

*Experience
Tension: pull or stretch
Slinky stretch
Tug-o-war fun
Standards: Focuses on task at hand even when frustrated or challenged
Developmental Domain/s: cognitive

Concept: 2
Forces that act upon bridges:
Tension and Compression

*Experience
Strong Shapes – trestles, trusses, and cantilevers exploring shape and strength
Standards:
Explores relation between words and meaning
Developmental Domain/s: cognitive, motor

Experience: Build a bridge
Standards: Develops, initiate sand carries out simple plans to obtain a goal
Developmental Domain/s: all

Concept: 3
Function/ Geography

*Experience: What does it span?
Explore the geographical phenomena spanned by bridges
Standards: Uses words acquired through conversations and shared reading (vocabulary)
Observes closely
Developmental Domain/s: cognitive

*Experience: Which is best? Examine the location and function of a bridge to determine which type of bridge will work best.
Standards: Explains reasoning for the solution selected & uses drawings to add detail to verbal descriptions
Developmental Domain/s: motor, cognitive

*Experience: Who uses bridges? Identify & map the bridges children encounter in everyday life.
Standards: Describes familiar people, places, things and experiences
Developmental Domain/s: motor, social, cognitive

Additional areas of study:
Builders/engineers
Bridge vocabulary
Team work/interaction with peers
Gaining information from text /reading comprehension

Once high quality experiences were identified then teachers referred to their assessment data related to content standards, developmental domains and IEP goals and objectives. They considered their *ACCESS Classroom Tracking Sheets* (ACTS) (see Figure 6-3) and other data and determined which content standards, developmental skills and IEP items were best addressed with the experience.

Figure 6-2: Excerpt from the ACTS

Language and Literacy Development

Students:	1	2	3	4	5
STRAND: Listening and Speaking					
Topic: Receptive Language and Comprehension					
Asks meaning of words	X	X	X	X	
Follows 2 step directions	X		X	X	
Understands complex concepts	X		X		X
Understands sentences (increasing length)				X	
Topic: Expressive Language					
Uses language to:					
express ideas		X	X	X	X
share observations	X		X	X	X
problem solve					
predict	X		X	X	X
seek information					
express ideas and feelings	X		X		X
describe familiar people, places , things	X		X		X
Uses drawing/visuals to support language	X			X	
Grammar:					
Uses nouns to describe					
forms regular plurals	X	X	X	X	
Understands & uses interrogatives					
Understands & uses prepositions					
Produces & expands complete sentences					
Vocabulary:					
Understands new words acquired through print					
Understands new words from variety settings	X	X	X	X	X
Connects words and use	X				
Explores relations between word meaning	X		X	X	
Adapted from the Ohio Department of Education, 2013					

The teachers noted that many experiences could be adjusted to better address the strengths, needs and interests of the children. For example, while working on Science Concept 1—Types of Bridges, the teachers were planning an experience, Beam Bridges, that addressed not only the science concept but also addressed the students' ability to work together cooperatively which is a developmental skill; identify/describe/create shapes which is a math standard and determines the meaning of new words in context of play which is a language arts standard (see Figure 6-3).

Figure 6-3: Science Concept Planner–Concept 1

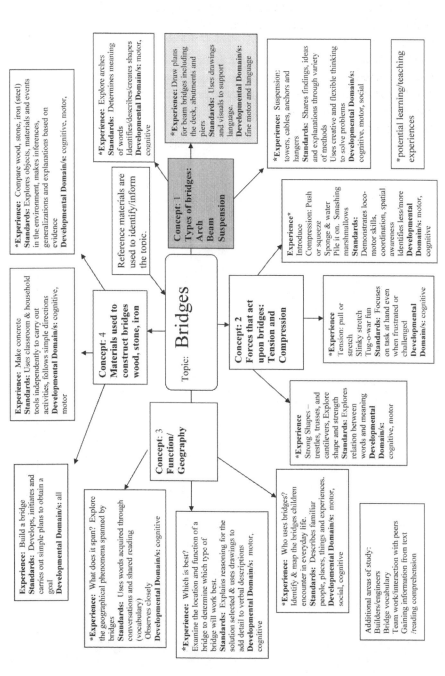

Note: *This figure can be found at www.ACCESScurriculum.com for easier viewing.*

While considering the language arts standards, the teachers determined that they could either have the children draw their observations or use emergent writing skills to begin to write symbols, letters or words to represent their observations. After examining the data on the ACTS, the teachers determined that most of the children were well practiced in talking about their experiences but many needed more practice to use drawings and visuals to support their language. These assessment data informed not only a planning decision but also led the teachers to systematically plan to assess the children's drawings which also included fine motor skill development. Many of the children were typically developing in their fine motor skills and so their development would be assessed on an annotated check sheet for the Bridges Investigation that included not only their expressive language skills but also included such fine motor skills as pencil grasp and hand dominance. One child in the group was not typically developing and had an Individualized Education Program (IEP) which included a goal and objectives related to fine motor development. The teachers adjusted the experience to address this child's IEP goal and included the goal in their documentation form (see Figure 6-4). By intentionally planning the experience using the *Science Concept Planner* and the ACTS, the teachers were able to address the children's interests, strengths and needs and also differentiate instruction to meet the needs of all learners in the classroom.

ACCESS has been developed to encourage intentionality and reflective teaching. Teachers who plan collaboratively using the planning process and aggregated assessment system find that they become highly engaged creators of meaningful curriculum. One comment that teachers make before they become accustomed to the *ACCESS* planning process is that content standards, developmental skills and IEP goals can be addressed without identifying an important topic to study. What is shown on figure 6-4 is common in classrooms that begin with content standards and lists of developmental skills to be addressed. Figure 6-4 depicts a scattered and disconnected approach to curriculum that is common in both preschool and primary classrooms.

Figure 6-4 Planning Without a Unifying Topic of Study

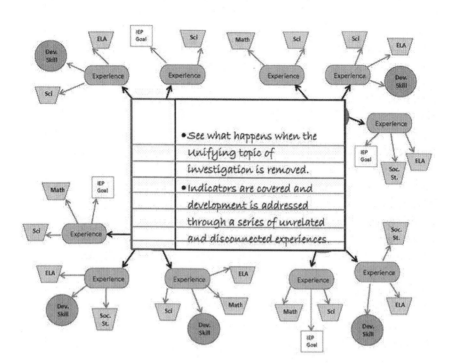

In figure 6-5 the teachers brainstormed possible experiences to support Science Concept 2. After referring to the ACTS, they found content indicators that were a good match for the experiences. They also noted that one experience supported a developmental skill but as written, only slightly addressed a content standard. The teachers discussed eliminating the experience but decided that it was important to the overall understanding of the science concept. They then decided to include the experience by adding props to the water table and using the opportunity to work with the children to introduce the concept of compression as they interacted with the water table, sponges and water (see Figure 6-5).

Figure 6-5 Science Concept Planner-Concept 2

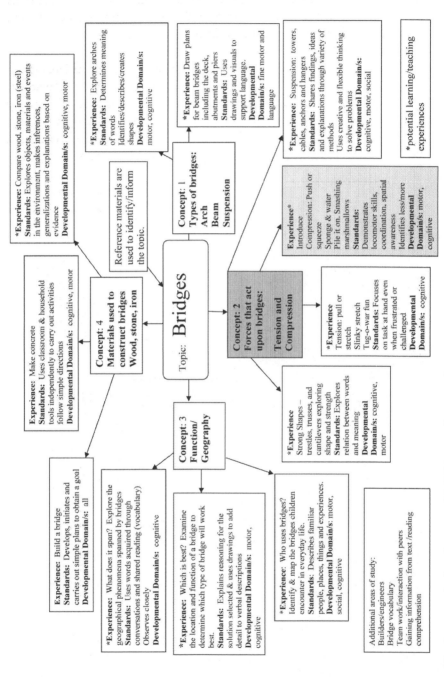

Note: This figure can be found at www.ACCESScurriculum.com for easier viewing.

Once again, decisions about instruction were made by focusing on the science concepts first and referring to the assessment data to make decisions about the environment, domains to be addressed, and content standards to include. A similar process is used for Concepts 3 and 4.

The science concept planner can be used to plan not only prekindergarten investigations but also investigation for the kindergarten-primary classroom. A real-life example is the investigation developed by, Nathan, a University of Dayton graduate student. Nathan developed an investigation on light for his student teaching and used it first in a preschool setting. He later revised the planner to include experiences and content appropriate for his second grade classroom experience. Nathan first identified 3 major concepts of light appropriate for the age group: Concept 1: Light sources are all around us, Concept 2: When something or someone blocks light, a shadow is formed and Concept 3: Light can be reflected (see Figure 6-6).

A prediction chart can be used with many investigations including a study of light

181

Figure 6-6: Nathan's Science Concept Planner—Light

LIGHT

When something, or someone, blocks light a shadow is formed.

Light sources are all around us and in nature.

Light can be reflected.

Experience: Guess That Shadow Interactive Read-aloud
Assessment: Checklist, Anecdotal Notes
Standards: ELAII 19, ELAII 34, S 12

Experience: What Creates this Shadow?
Assessment: Checklist, Anecdotal Notes
Standards: S 12, S 15, SS 13

Experience: Shadow Scavenger Hunt
Assessment: Anecdotal Notes, Photos
Standards: ELAI 31, ELAII 26, ELAII 30, S 3

Experience: Shadow Animal Theatre
Assessment: Checklist, Anecdotal Notes, Photos
Standards: ELAI 31, ELAII 34, S 1, SS 12

Experience: Cave Introduction
Assessment: Anecdotal Notes
Standards: ELAII 31, ELAII 34, S 13

Experience: Shadow Tracing
Assessment: Checklist, Anecdotal Notes, Work Samples, Photos
Standards: ELAI 15, ELAI 28, ELAI 30, S 14, SS 12

Experience: Reflection Prediction
Assessment: Checklist, Anecdotal Notes, Work Samples, Photos
Standards: ELAI 28, ELAII 26, S 12, SHPS 14

Experience: Cave Center
Assessment: Checklist, Anecdotal Notes, Photos
Standards: ELAI 1, ELA1 25, S 3, S 30, SS 7

Experience: Light Source Discussion
Assessment: Checklist, Anecdotal Notes, Photos
Standards: ELAII 13, ELAII 27, ELAII 31, M 7, M 8, M 9, M 37, S 4, SS 9

Experience: Flashlight Center
Assessment: Anecdotal Notes, Video
Standards: ELAI 25, ELAII 27, S 6, S 30, SS 12

Experience: I See Myself Interactive Read-Aloud
Assessment: Checklist, Anecdotal Notes, Photos
Standards: ELAII 9, ELAII 27, ELAII 29, M 34, S 3, S 26, SS 27

Experience: Light Scavenger Hunt
Assessment: Anecdotal Notes, Work Samples, Photos
Standards: ELAI 1, ELAI 12, ELAII 9, S 14, S 30, SHPS 24

Experience: Flashlight Circle Time
Assessment: Checklist, Anecdotal Notes, Photos
Standards: M 1, S 24, SHPS 24, SS 12

Experience: Bear Hunt with Flashlights
Assessment: Checklist, Anecdotal Records
Standards: ELAI 30, ELAII 10, M 36

Experience: Light Collage
Assessment: Checklist, Anecdotal Notes, Work Sample
Standards: ELAII 2, S 11, SHPS 18, SS 10

Experiences were then developed that were developmentally appropriate, with modifications included for children in the classroom who needed additional support. By writing out the experiences, Nate was able to determine needed materials, sequence of concepts, and anticipated timing. He then addressed the Early Learning Content for the preschool class and his data from previous work with the children that he had recorded on a *ACCESS* Class Tracking Sheet or ACTS shown early in chapter, and determined standards that would best be met in his experiences. Data collection on all of the experiences helped Nate determine next steps in his instruction or if modifications were required.

Figure 6-7: Nathan's Lesson Plan

Name: Nathan Henderson	**Lesson Title:** Light Scavenger Hunt
Date: 01-28-11	**Grade Level**: Preschool Special Education
Indicators: ELAI 1, ELAI 12, ELAII 9, S 14, S 30, SHPS 24*	
Developmental Domains: Aesthetic, Cognitive, Physical	
Accommodations: Morning: 1) Provide Jack S. with models and cues to follow simple instructions and participate in routines. 2) Provide Damien with specific modeling of 3-4 syllable words and /s/ and /f/. 3) Provide Bryce with modeling of beginning consonant sounds and introduce new nouns and facilitate practice of pronunciation. 4) Provide Brianna with modeling and cues to produce blends, multi-syllable words, and proper breath and rate of speech. 5) Try to speak towards Blake's right ear. Afternoon: 1) Provide Kylie with modeling of words with blends. 2) Provide Josh with modeling and pronunciation opportunities with /s/ and /f/. 3) Assist Autumn in practicing listening skills and opportunities to follow simple instructional commands requiring a response. 4) Assist Trent with focusing his attention on the experience at hand and with displaying appropriate behavior. 5) Provide Emily with cues to follow simple procedures. 6) Provide Alex and William with Spanish phrases and words to help them make a connection to the material and learn English.	

*This investigation was planned using the standards that were available in 2011 when it was developed.

Instructional Objectives	Assessment of Student Learning	Learning Experiences
Objectives: The students will be able to . . . 1) Identify several light sources. 2) Point out own name in a list. 3) "Print" left to right. 4) Describe attributes. 5) Engage in simple scientific inquiry, records data. 6) Explore familiar sources of light. 7) Use drawing tools with ease.	**Identify Evidence:** Anecdotal Records, Work Samples, Photographs **Aggregate/Compile Evidence:** One educator will record anecdotal notes and help the students take pictures of the light sources. Following the lesson, the educator will review the work samples and anecdotal notes to assess the children's learning of the instructional objectives. The educator will compile all of that data onto a larger whole class check sheet as part of an ongoing assessment of each student's progress.	(This learning experience will be conducted over 2 to 3 days) **Day 1** 1. As a whole group the educator will review various sources of light with the children. 2. Following the review, the students will split into 4 small groups of 3 or 4 students each. One group at a time will take part in the scavenger hunt. The other 3 groups will take part in free play and other learning experiences. 3. The educator will assemble a group and explain that they will take a short walk around the school and observe objects in the school that produce light. 4. After the educator introduces the purpose of the experience, they will give each student a science journal and writing device. 5. The educator will lead the students down through the halls and into any rooms previously cleared by other educators and school staff. As the group explores each area, the educator facilitates discussion about sources of light and ask the students to record their observations with pictures and writing. 6. The educator and students will return to the classroom and begin the experience with another group.

	Interpret the Evidence: Based on the students' drawings and anecdotal records all of the children were able to identify light sources and record their observations and fulfill the objectives for this lesson. Of note, all of the students were able to locate their journals based on their own writing or the educator's writing on the back of the journal. Also, most of the children were able to print their names from left to right.	**Day 2** 1. Following morning group routine, the educator will hand out the students' science journals and will conduct a 5 minute discussion with the students sharing their observations. (If time does not allow for all groups to participate in the experience on day 1, then an additional day will be provided for all groups to participate.) **Educator Roles:** One educator will lead the students on the scavenger hunt. During the scavenger hunt two educators will engage the students in free play and other learning experiences. During whole group portions, one educator will lead the discussion, one educator will record student observations and comments, and one educator will monitor students and Remind, Redirect, and Remove, as well as provide additional support if the students appear lost.

Resources:
- Science Journals
- Writing Devices (preferably pen to avoid broken pencil lead)
- Digital Camera

Reflection:

The light scavenger hunt experience turned out to be a big success. The children thoroughly enjoyed exploring the school and searching for light sources. We were also able to further solidify the students' understanding of the light sources when they found an item that was not a light source. And oddly enough the children absolutely were enthralled when I introduced the science journals and explained that while we will be using these for science and keeping them at school for the next three weeks, the science journals were theirs to keep. Probably the hardest part of the whole experience was collecting the science journals after we were done.

We conducted the scavenger hunt during free play and center time so we could take smaller groups around the school. Initially I selected groups with a mix of ages and abilities but quickly selected more homogenous grouping after the first two excursions. I thought that the mixture of children would allow the children with a better grasp of the concept to help the other students, but everyone was so focused on the hunt that they did not have the time to help other students. And some of the younger children were understandably ready to return to the classroom and begin another activity while some of the more advanced students wanted to continue on the hunt. Making the switch to more homogenous groups allowed us to customize each hunt more appropriately. In fact we took one group out for over forty-five minutes.

Before Mrs. Humrick and I took the children out on the hunt, I passed out a science journal and pen to each student. A lot of educators have different ideas about pens versus pencils, but for this activity I chose pens. Not only do children seem to worry less about making mistakes, but also I do not have to worry about them breaking the pencil lead. However, next time I will make sure to buy some better pens, because occasionally these pens would stop writing, or the children would have to press so hard that their papers ripped.

First I asked them to write their names on the journal. Each student was eager to write his/her name, and it provided me with an opportunity to assess their concepts of print and basic writing skills. Plus they were excited to make the journals their own. I also wrote every student's name on the back so everyone else could tell whose journal was whose.

I wanted to callback to our light source discussion, so I added a quick review of the "light source" and "not a light source" pictures cards to the lesson. I would definitely add this to a future edition of this particular experience. The children were able to make connections and refresh the still new idea of light sources.

The scavenger hunt itself went swimmingly, and the children were so engaged that we did not have any behavior issues other than some of the younger children getting antsy in the first two groups. The children especially enjoyed being able to hold the digital camera and take their own pictures. The children especially enjoyed exploring the kindergarten wing. The best room we found was the teacher's lounge, since there were unique light sources aplenty. Unfortunately, we did get the stink eye from two teachers taking a break, but tough, they should enjoy watching young children learn! I actually received a lot of positive feedback from other staff members on how they enjoyed watching the children run through the halls excitedly identifying light sources.

The one issue was that a lot of the students would identify a light source but then state, "I can't do it," or, "I can't draw it." The self-confidence to attempt a drawing was not present. I resisted the urge to model drawing, and instead pointed out features and shapes in the objects. Eventually if their anxiousness to draw was overpowering their focus on light sources. I did try to help them by modeling how to draw a particular object in their notebook. Another unexpected issue was that many children were so excited to keep finding light sources that they would make a quick scribble or doodle and move on. I had to slow them down by asking to look at the light source and add more details to their picture. Also, I once again forgeo to take pictures because I was too engaged in the scavenger hunt.

Contributed by Nathan Henderson, 2011

Many teachers express fear of using a science topic as the center of their curriculum. The fear is that not all content areas can be adequately addressed. Take a few moments to work on Nate's concept web. What experiences can you think of that will allow the children to learn the concept? Then, what content standards can be identified that go with the experiences? As has been evidenced here, all content areas can and are included in an extended investigation. Extended investigations, as stated in an earlier chapter, also allow children to demonstrate their knowledge and skills while highlighting the need for the development of new skills. In order to share information or record their exciting discoveries in their journals, children need to be able to write or draw. As children identify this real life need for a skill, they are motivated to learn and practice this skill. Teachers can assess children's skills and understanding in authentic situations and use that knowledge to plan curriculum incorporating all content areas.

Other teachers may be hesitant to use a science topic as the center of their curriculum for fear they would not have the science knowledge needed to conduct an in depth investigation. For those teachers, they might want to start with a familiar topic such as apples but with a different twist on the traditional coloring of apple handouts. A visit to an orchard for a hay ride and having an apple for snack could introduce the topic. Thinking deeper, students and the teacher could explore the concepts of how apples grow, the life cycle including what happens when an apple rots, what are the many uses for apples and what is the relationship between apples and insects. Concepts of energy exchange and change of matter could be introduced as students discover what happens when apples are heated. Comparisons of the many types of apples and the differences in texture, uses, and taste could be made. Content standards from all domains including science, social studies, mathematics and language arts can easily be identified and documented as the children participate in experiences that will help answer key questions.

Investigations with Infants and Toddlers

Addressing science topics with infants and toddlers is easier than it may seem. Taking everyday activities such as cooking or gardening can create a whole world of investigation for very young children who are trying to make sense of the world. Beginning with the children's interests and environment, teachers can make learning opportunities out of everyday experiences. When children are outside, for example, they notice things like trees, flowers, and other plants. Taking this idea and creating a science investigation can give very young children many opportunities for authentic learning in a familiar environment. Growing vegetables and flowers is a way for teachers to intentionally develop skills across all domains as seen in the following learning web (see figure 6-8).

Figure 6-8 Infant and Toddler Learning Experience

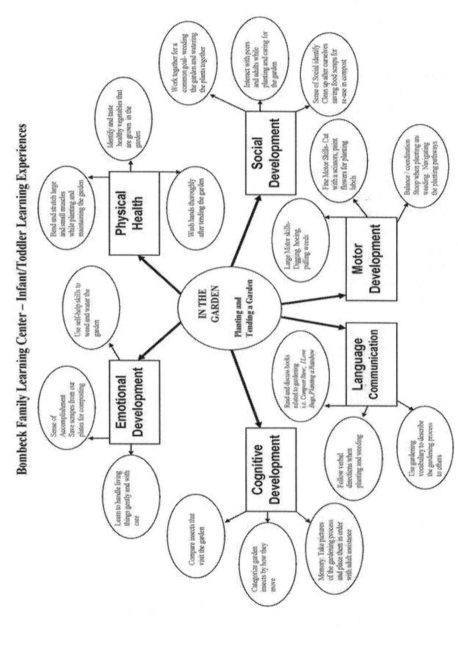

Bombeck Family Learning Center – Infant/Toddler Learning Experiences

Note: This Figure can be found at www.ACCESScurriculum.com for easier viewing.

Using gardening as an intentional investigation with very young children can become an ongoing project as teachers and children work together to grow flowers and vegetables and use them in daily lesson plans. Investigations should begin by recognizing student needs through assessment tools that are age appropriate. At the Bombeck Center, teachers use the Ages and Stages Questionnaire (ASQ) (Squires & Bricker 2009) as a formal assessment to track milestones in infant and toddler development. Teachers also use authentic documentation processes like photographs and anecdotal notes that depict a child's strengths and weaknesses and are compiled into a portfolio binder that aligns with the Early Learning and Development Standards for infants and toddlers.

Communication with parents and family is also a key part of identifying a child's individual needs. As infants and toddlers, many children are developing similar skills such as fine and gross motor, language, cognitive, and most importantly, social and emotional. When children have strong emotional bonds early in life through established relationships and routines, it helps them create a sense of self in the world and lays the foundation for executive functioning, learning and well balanced social and emotional development. Very young children can begin to be comfortable and make connections from their everyday routines to learning goals aligned with developmental domains and core standards as teachers create intentional learning experiences surrounding children's interests.

By using students' interests and pre-assessment tools, teachers can then begin to determine what activities will appropriately address their students' needs across all developmental domains. With an investigation about gardening, students with special needs for fine motor development can be addressed through planting. Picking up seeds with a pincer grasp and pushing them into the dirt helps with fine motor control and cognitive skills like following directions. Pre-writing skills are also addressed through fine motor activities like drawing and painting what toddlers see in their environment as their garden grows. As the vegetables and berries grow, children learn to pick them and understand how plants produce food, which addresses science and social studies standards, even as infants and toddlers. Many opportunities are provided to expose young children to new vocabulary and elicit language skills as teachers continue the gardening investigation. Labeling the plants and foods that are in the garden with pictures and words helps children connect literacy to pictures as well as encourages them to try new vocabulary like "soil, seedling, stem," and other garden related words as they learn to speak. While implementing these authentic learning experiences, teachers are focused on each child's needs as they go through the daily routines and specific lessons outlined in their planning web. Integrating developmental domains and common cores standards with infants and toddlers can become part of the classroom daily routine when teachers are intentional in their planning and implementation of investigation topics.

Chapter Summary

In summary, the need to integrate content standards with developmental skills, and sometimes IEP goals is not a hard concept if teachers are willing to step out of the traditional model and acknowledge to the children that they too have questions on topics of study such as, "do worms really eat through apples?" As a side note, the answer is no, unless the egg was laid in the bloom of the apple. Content standards from all areas can easily be included in investigations and experiences by first identifying what children know, using assessment data, and then identifying what children need to know. Data sheets in the form of check sheets, portfolio sheets or annotated check sheets can help teachers document what each child has mastered, as well as what has been addressed in the classroom setting as the year progresses.

ACCESS Steps for Success: Integrating Standards

1. Teachers plan and stage environments to inspire young children to play, to think, and to engage in inquiry.
2. Teachers observe children to determine areas of interest.
3. Teachers analyze possible topics for investigation ensuring that they are worthy of study, reflect the interests of children and are broad enough to support learning and development.
4. Teachers brainstorm to complete a science concept planner, or if working with infants and/or toddlers, learning experience planner.
5. Teachers connect curriculum in meaningful ways by selecting content standards from several disciplines and developmental domains, making sure to include children's IEP goals. Infant and toddler teachers should focus on developmental skills.
6. Teachers create and use authentic assessment tools to add data to the ACTS.
7. Teachers plan future investigations and learning experiences around assessment results, integrating standards and developmental skills across the curriculum.

References

Association for Supervision and Curriculum Development (2004). *Planning and organizing for curriculum renewal.* Author.

Garelick, B. (Nov. 20, 2012). A new kind of problem: The Common Core Math Standards. *The Atlantic.com.*

Katz, L. G., & Chard, S. C. (1998). Issues in selecting topics for projects. *ERIC Clearinghouse on Elementary and Early Childhood Education/ ERIC Digest:* ED424031.

National Governors Association Center for Best Practices & Council of Chief State School Officers. (2010). *Common Core State Standards.* Washington, DC: Authors.

Newton, X., (2007). Reflections on math reforms in the U.S.: A cross-national perspective." *Education Digest: Essential Readings Condensed for Quick Review,* Vol. 73, Issue 1.

Ohio Department of Education (2013). *Ohio Early Learning and Development Standards.* Columbus, OH: Author.

Squires, J. & Bricker, D. (2009). *Ages & Stages Questionnaires[R], Third Edition (ASQ-3[TM]): A Parent-Completed Child-Monitoring System.* Baltimore, MD: Brookes.

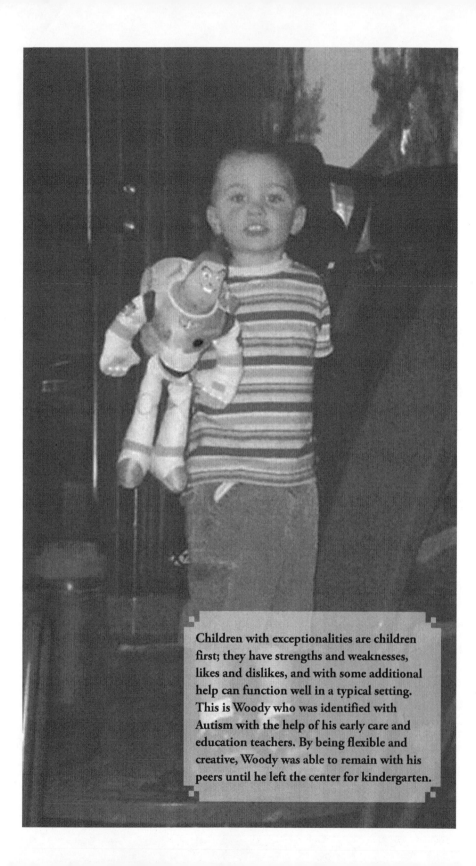

Children with exceptionalities are children first; they have strengths and weaknesses, likes and dislikes, and with some additional help can function well in a typical setting. This is Woody who was identified with Autism with the help of his early care and education teachers. By being flexible and creative, Woody was able to remain with his peers until he left the center for kindergarten.

7

Including Children with Exceptionalities

- *The concept of inclusion means different things to different individuals, and it is rooted in values, evidence-based practice, community standards, and personal experience (Larocque & Darling, 2008, p. 3).*
- *Developmentally Appropriate Practice is, by definition, individually appropriate as well as age appropriate. A program cannot possibly achieve individual appropriateness without assessing and planning for children's individual needs and interests (Bredekamp, 1993, p. 263).*

The notion of exceptionalities in young children varies widely from setting to setting. Some would think of a child they knew who was developing motor or language skills slowly, while others think of children with genetic disorders such as Down syndrome, or physically involved children with cerebral palsy. The severity of the disability affects beliefs about who can be served in child care settings, preschools, or general education classes. However, children are children; they have likes and dislikes, have unique personalities, and develop at their own pace, regardless of a disability. This chapter will provide some background on the education of young children with exceptionalities and will help integrate all of the content learned in the previous chapters into application of *ACCESS* for children with exceptionalities.

A Brief History

The history of the education of young children identified with, or at-risk for, disabilities began in the 1960's with model demonstration programs that were designed to identify successful strategies for improving developmental skills, however, there were few of these federally funded programs with a limited number of children being served. Laws passed in the 1970's, especially P.L. 94-142 the Education for All Handicapped Children's Act, provided all children ages of 6-18 the right to attend school. Children age 3-5 were also to be served if the state served other children of that age group. In 1986, with PL 99-457, an amendment to PL94-142, it became mandatory that children with exceptionalities ages three to five be identified and served by local school agencies with a suggestion that states also develop programs for children ages birth to three years. This resulted in the start of separate classrooms for young children with exceptionalities, sometimes in schools, often in rehabilitation facilities or community settings such as church basements. Integration with typical peers was not part of these programs which focused on remediation of deficits through therapy and education.

The earliest classrooms for young children with exceptionalities functioned on a behaviorist model of learning. The key components included learning evidenced by observable change in behavior which had been shaped by the environment and increased with reinforcement. Individual skills were chosen, and the child engaged in trials to learn the content i.e. sorting—if the child put the red blocks in the red bowl they received praise and/or a tangible reward. The theory was that providing reinforcement would increase the likelihood of the behavior happening again (Merriam & Cafffarella, 1999). Tasks were determined by the developmental level of the child and addressed deficit skill areas. This model of instruction led to the learning of individual skills but not within the context of a topic that would provide content knowledge for the isolated task.

Paired with this model was a combination of techniques/strategies that came from the early demonstration models such as High Scope or the Frank Porter Graham Child Development Institute at the University of North Carolina—Chapel Hill. High Scope provided the structure for the environment and classroom using daily routines. The FPG Institute along with the Carolina Curriculum for Preschoolers with Special Needs provided assessment and curriculum insight. Children were assessed on the skills expected for their age and then goals and objectives were developed for each child's IEP.

A "typical" early childhood special needs classroom had a schedule that included table top activities for language and fine motor skills; circle time for language, cognition, and social skills: snack for all developmental skills; gross motor time; and individual or small group work stations for each child to work on needed skills. Generally a theme was chosen for the week such as farm animals, transportation vehicles, fruits and vegetables, and circle and art projects focused on this theme. Another option was the "letter of the week" model, where a letter was introduced at circle and carried out throughout the snack, art, and as many other activities as possible. For example: for the letter H, there would be a story about Happy Harry, the art project would include the letter H with coloring, gluing, developing Hs, snack would discuss H foods such as hamburger, ham, honey with tasting of the food if possible. Motor skills would continue with the theme focusing on hopping stories/ book reading also related to H with words such as hippopotamus, home, happy, etc. Connections between content was not evident, and authentic activities were limited as well. H books would be fiction story books designed to address language skills instead of non-fiction books to address content. This type of classroom structure continued for years, and unfortunately many programs for children with exceptionalities continue theme-based curriculums i.e. Circus, farm animals, butterflies, letter-of-the-week based, or story-based weeks that allow for exposure to topics but not in-depth exploration and development for any of the children in the class.

Revisions of the Individuals with Disabilities Education Act (IDEA) in 1997or the Education for All Handicapped Act until 1990 required all children have access to the general education curriculum. For young children this meant the Early Learning Content Standards developed in most states in addition to addressing traditional developmental skills. Inclusive classrooms were strongly recommended, and in some states required, with typically developing peers serving as models for classmates with disabilities. This resulted in adding "typical" peers to classrooms but did not always change the model of instruction.

During this development of ECSE classrooms, the Division for Early Childhood (DEC) was formed as a division of CEC (Council for Exceptional Children). The mission of DEC is to "[promote] policies and [advance] evidence-based practices that support families and enhance the optimal development of young children who have or are at risk for developmental delays and disabilities" (*DEC*, nd). As DEC evolved with the research and practices of serving young children with special needs and their families, they developed a set of "Recommended Practices," published in 1993. However, per Sandall, Hemmeter, Smith, and McLean (2005), these were not widely known or utilized. Thus, a significant revision and efforts to disseminate the "Recommended Practices" occurred in the early 2000's. To begin, DEC focused on the recommended practices for all children offered through the National Association for the Education of Young Children and Head Start Program Performance Standards. The concepts of Developmentally Appropriate Practices were recognized as fundamental for all organizations serving young children. This basically meant, per Bredekamp & Copple (1997), that individuals making decisions about caring for and educating children had to take into consideration what was known about child development and learning, what was known about the strengths, interests and needs of individual children, and knowledge of the social and cultural context in which children live. The DEC *Recommended Practices were* "[built] on and extend[ed] this foundation of quality programs for all children in order to meet the specific needs of children with disabilities" (Sandal, et al., 2005, p. 25). DEC also determined some basic values for their organization, including:

- Respect for all children and families
- Services and supports which were comprehensive, coordinated, and family-centered
- Rights for all children to participate actively and meaningfully within their families and communities (Sandal, et al., 2005, p. 21-23).

With an increasing knowledge of how children learn, Childress (2004) reflects that intervention services have changed "from a service-based, professional-driven approach that has focused on deficits and needs to a supportive approach emphasizing child and family strengths and natural routines . . ." (p. 163). With these changes has also come a change in the way children with exceptionalities are served in early care and education settings. The behaviorist model that had been used was gradually changing to more of a constructivist approach with children given the opportunity to build upon their current knowledge through engaging in experiences. Integrating children with special needs into inclusive classrooms provided more role models and opportunities to engage in authentic learning experiences. The move to an intentional, inquiry-based teaching model with integration of content standards and IEP goal through *ACCESS,* reflects best practices recommended by DEC and NAEYC.

Recommended Practices for
Young Children with Exceptionalities

(DEC Guidelines)

The 2005 published version of the *DEC Recommended Practices* places an emphasis on research, promising practices, and administrative and systems change. Components of the *Recommended Practices* include direct service strands: assessment, child-focused practices, family-based practices, interdisciplinary models, and technology applications. Indirect supports strands include policies, procedures, systems change, and personnel preparation (Sandall et al., 2005). A discussion of how *ACCESS* corresponds with *DEC Recommended Practices* follows.

Assessment

Chapter 2 of this book discussed the Assessment methods to be used for all young children as those that are "developmentally appropriate, culturally and linguistically responsive, tied to children's daily activities, supported by professional development, and inclusive of families" (NAEYC/NAECS/SDE, 2003, p. 2). In addition, Chapter 2 discusses Neisworth and Bagnato's article (2004) that supports an authentic assessment model which utilizes the child's natural environment and daily activities to provide the information required to make decisions about young children's developmental levels and/or programmatic needs. While this is true for all children, Neisworth and Bagnato (2004) worked with DEC to develop eight assessment related standards which are tied to the *DEC Recommended Practices* for assessment of children with exceptionalities. Six of the eight standards directly refer to instruments both formal and informal, used in preschool settings. They include the usefulness of the instrument, the acceptability of the tool by professionals and families, the use of natural methods and context, the adaptability for children with exceptionalities, the consideration of all ecological data in the interpretation of the results, and professional/parent collaboration.

Neisworth and Bagnato's (2004) assessment related standards are as follows:

- **Utility**—Assessments must be useful to help determine needs and possible intervention strategies. Monitoring progress of the child and suitability of the program are also goals of assessment, thus assessments must be useful for those tasks as well. Assessments must also have "treatment validity" (Sandall, et al., 2005) which means a connection between program goals, developmental skills, and child objectives.
- **Acceptability**—Families and professionals must agree on the methods, styles, and materials being used for the assessment. The methods must be worthwhile and able to detect changes in behavior seen by parents or care-givers.
- **Authenticity**—Materials, the people involved, and the place of the assessment must be typically where and what the child is familiar with. Using non-familiar toys, with an unfamiliar person, in a strange setting will not result in positive results on the assessment.
- **Collaboration**—The assessment must engage parents and family members as well as the child. Parents or other care givers have the knowledge of the child's overall development, thus a collaborative assessment is essential to determine the real strengths and needs of the child.
- **Convergence**—All information must be considered from parents, care-givers, and others. Converging all of this information will provide a total picture of the child, again allowing a more natural picture of the child's abilities.
- **Equity**—Assessments must follow the rules of non-discriminatory testing. Sensory needs, culture, response modes and language must all be considered when determining if an assessment is equitable.
- **Sensitivity**—Assessment tools must have appropriate content validity with enough assessing items at each developmental level to notice even the smallest change.
- **Congruence**—The assessment and materials used must have been validated on the types of children who are going to be assessed. There must be congruency to be able to use the assessment to determine strengths and weaknesses (Sandall et al., 2005).

ACCESS follows these standards. Since the assessments designed are directly related to early learning content standards and/or IEP goals, they definitely meet the standard of **utility**; the purpose is to monitor the progress of the child, and the curriculum of the program. As the assessments are developed with the program goals, the connection between the program, the content and the child's objectives are easily met. The assessment system used in *ACCESS* is developed by the families and staff of the centers. As they have developed what they are using,(based on content standards and IEP goals, it is generally considered **acceptable. Authenticity** is stressed in the investigations, thus the assessments will also be authentic, and **collaboration** with other staff members, the children, and their parents is a part of the planning process. *ACCESS* provides for a **convergence** of assessment forms, including daily check sheets, IEP goals, anecdotal records and observations.

Equity can be considered met when the investigations are designed to allow all children to participate at their level. For example, while older children are mixing paint to determine primary and secondary colors, younger children or those with exceptionalities could be working on color identification, use of fine motor skills, or sharing the paint. **Sensitivity** and **congruence** appear more related to standardized assessments although since the investigations and assessments are designed to meet the needs of the children, it could be argued that it is sensitive to the individual gains of the children.

Child-Focused Practices

Per DEC, "Child-Focused Practices include the decisions and strategies used to structure and provide learning opportunities for children" (Wolery in Sandall, et al., 2005, p. 71). The goals of Early Intervention/Early Childhood Special Education (EI/ECSE) include promoting the child's learning and development, increasing a child's interactions with the social and physical environment, and using research supported instructional techniques to increase the developmental skills and interaction with others and the environment. Adults are charged with:

- Designing environments to promote safety, active engagement, learning participation and membership
- Using ongoing data to individualize and adapt practices to meet the needs of the child

- Using systematic procedures within and across environments, activities, and routines to promote learning and participation (Sandall, et al., 2005, p.73).

ACCESS believes in a child-centered model of instruction, which allows for all of the recommended practices listed above. Each child participates at his/her own level, striving for the next step in development and learning. Children with exceptionalities are children first, and expectations to participate and improve skills and knowledge are evident for all children. The environment is designed for varying levels of abilities as are the investigations and experiences. Inquiry based learning (NIEER Preschool Policy Brief, Mar 2009) has been proven to expand a child's learning, engagement, and participation/membership in the classroom.

Teachers using *ACCESS* design environments to facilitate learning and active engagement of the children. Small groups encourage learning participation and membership with children helping each other and sharing materials regardless of a disability. Data is collected on every child during the investigations and activities of daily routines which are then used to record growth and progress for planning the next experiences for the children. This intentional planning allows for maximum use of time and active engagement of all children.

Children help each other in a strong community, regardless of ability levels

Children working together improve social skills and develop a sense of membership in the classroom.

Family-based Practices

Family-based practices include the provision of resources and supports thus allowing families to have the time, energy, knowledge, and skills, to provide learning experiences and opportunities for their child (Tirvette & Dunst in Sandall, et al., 2005). To allow this to happen, parents and early childhood staff must share responsibility and collaborate to develop goals and achieve desired outcomes. Family functioning must also be strengthened to facilitate "typical" family development and activities regardless of the need to include a child with exceptionality. Family-based practices also include the willingness and ability to allow parents to take the lead on what they want to work on with their child. The family's values must be considered when intervention practices are being developed and implemented.

The data system and on-going evaluation of what the child is doing in the classroom, provides immediate access to parents who want to know how their child is doing in the program or maybe just on a specific skill. This information can be taken to other professionals, such as the child's doctor, therapists, or other care agents. Parents can also have data sheets to keep at home to mark down what the child does on specific goals in the home. As this is a dynamic system, the child has the opportunity to return to skills and concepts frequently which allows for greater possibility of mastery of skills before moving on to the next activity. Faculty and staff can work with the parents to ensure they are comfortable with the skill they want the child to learn and where to go next once that skill has been mastered.

ACCESS brings in "experts," often the parents, to help the children in their various investigations. Parents are invited to share their skills and knowledge, and thus richer, deeper, and more cognitively aware experiences are available. In one preschool, a father who was an engineer, came in to help the children build the roof of the University chapel replica. The children and classroom staff could not make the copula stay on the roof. The father came and worked with the children, instead of doing it on his own, and the children completed a realistic replica of the University chapel. Another example is to use people in the community. During an investigation of rocks, one of the teachers called the "rock man," and he came to the school with various rocks, a working sluice to pan for rocks, and a display board where the children could compare their finds to determine the name of their rocks. Children with exceptionalities were included in both of these tasks at the level of their ability.

Providing a visual aid for the children allows for matching and comparisons and questions regarding the rocks.

Interdisciplinary Models of Instruction

Recommended practices also include the use of **interdisciplinary models**. This means all specialists and teachers working with the child, work together to help the child and his/her family. The model of **transdisciplinary** services refers to the specific ways team members interact. The transdisciplinary model "require[s] all professionals to collaborate and provide integrated routines-based interventions in children's natural environments" (Sandell, et al., 2005). *ACCESS* encourages natural environments and content embedded in daily routines. All children are expected to participate in daily routines, and that includes the child with exceptionalities. For example, signing into class could mean writing their name for some children, copying for others, or just scribbling. Signing in, no matter what form that takes, is a skill.

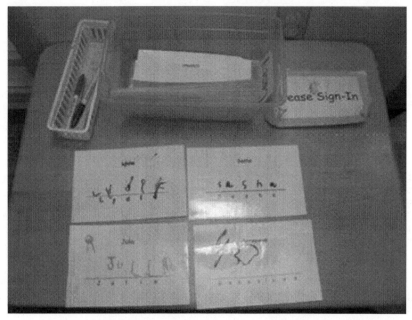

In this photo children are writing at all stages of development, but each child knows it is a daily routine to "sign-in" when they come to school.

Through either the interdisciplinary or transdisciplinary model, the therapist working with the child with exceptionalities will be in the classroom assisting the teachers. The teachers can plan an experience that allows the occupational therapist (OT) to work with the child beside his/her peers such as a cutting activity of making leaves for the tree the class is building. The OT could also position herself at the sign-in table to help as the child holds a crayon and "writes" his/her name. Pull-out therapy services are not recommended unless necessary based on individual's needs.

Technology Applications

The application of technology must be considered for every child who has an IEP/IFSP. This would include the three types of technology application: assistive, instructional/educational, and informational (Sandall et al. 2005). Assistive technology is defined as: "any item, piece of equipment, or product, whether acquired commercially, off the shelf, modified, or customized, that is used to increase, maintain, or improve the functional capabilities of individual with disabilities" (P.L. 100-407, the Technology-Related Assistance for Individuals with Disabilities Act of 1988). Technology can be either "high tech" like computers, Braille readers, environmental control units or "low tech" such as a pencil grip, Co-Writer, special chair, etc. All children in the classroom can benefit from the use of the technology regardless the identification of an exceptionality. BoardMaker can be used to make communication boards for around the classroom so the younger children can also use pictures to communicate if they have not yet learned the words. An IPad can be used as a communication board with the addition of *Go Talk Now* from Attainment Company, or science can come alive with the app from *Science 360*.

Use of the Internet to locate other resources, videotapes to show parents what a child has done in the classroom, a picture schedule, or a modified handle on a spoon are all examples of technology facilitating the learning and engagement of a child with exceptionalities.

Visual schedules can be helpful for one child to know where to go next, but a visual "centers" schedule can also be used for the whole class to help them know where they are scheduled to play/work.

ACCESS and RTI

As children enter the primary grades, those who are on IEPs will continue to receive support and engage in the integrated investigations by adding their IEP goals into the experiences just as in preschool. Teachers can take data on the IEP goals during daily routines such as the aforementioned "sign in." While some goals are content standards for early learners, the child with an exceptionality may continue to have objectives such as "can recognize own name in print," "writes from left to right and top to bottom on a page," or "identifies letters other than those in his/her name." Quick data on these goals can be taken during the sign-in time, providing direct instruction as needed and linking it to a daily routine. Other students, who may not be on IEPs, may need work on the same concepts. A small group can be formed to address the needs of children at-risk, non-English speaking learners, and for those with identified needs.

Often children do not demonstrate their diverse learning needs until they reach the primary grades. In recent years, the process of *response to intervention (RTI)* has helped to determine eligibility for special education for school aged children. According to The Council for Exceptional Children (CEC) RTI identifies struggling learners early, provides access to needed interventions, and helps identify children with disabilities. RTI is a process intended to assist in identifying children with disabilities by providing data about how a child responds to scientifically based intervention as part of the comprehensive evaluation required for any disability identification (CEC, 2008, p.1).

As described in Chapter 1, *ACCESS* is research based and is an excellent means of keeping data on all children in the classroom. The teacher can readily see who is having difficulties with a concept/standard by using the ACTS, and systematically taking data that allows for a quick review of the children and the standards. An example of quick data keeping might be the use of a slash [/] for documenting the introduction to a standard, an [X] for documenting that the child is demonstrating the standard sometimes, or using an asterisk [*] when the child has mastered the skill (see Figure 7-1). These children can then be moved on to the second tier of RTI, a more systematic approach to teaching needed skills. The *ACCESS* documentation checklists can be helpful at this level of RTI by providing data on individual students as well as standards and elements of the standards. A brief look allows the teacher to see who is in need of assistance with a learning content standard and/or developmental skill.

Figure 7-1 Observational Check sheets (OCs)   Bird Investigation

Indicator	Amy	Kyra	Logan	Emilee	Laura	Brian	Maddie	Jen	Jill	Kelly	Bill	Hank
Book Handling (ELA III 2,3) -Holds book upright -Turns pages from left to right -Distinguishes print from pictures	*	*	*	*	*	*	*	*	*	/	*	*
Interacts with and responds to guidance and assistance in socially accepted ways (SSV 1)	*	*	*	*	*	*		*	*	*	*	
Research (ELA IX 1, SV8) -Records findings -Asks questions	*	*	/	*	*	/	*	/	*	/	/	X
Explores objects, organisms and events using simple equipment (magnets, magnifiers, measuring tools) (SV6)	*	*	*	*	*	*		*	*	*	*	*
Engages in problem solving behavior with diminishing support	*	/	*	*	*	*		*	*	*	/	/
Demonstrates awareness of the outcomes of one's own choices (SSVI4)	X	*	X	*	*	X		X	X	X	*	/
Demonstrates increasing ability to make independent choices and follows through on plans (SS VI 3)												
Identifies common needs of familiar living things (food, air, water) SII 1	*	*	*	*	*	*	*	*	*	*	*	X
Recognizes the difference between helpful and harmful (S VI 2)												
Compares, observes, and represents changes over time in the natural environment SI 3,4,7	*	*	*	*	*	*	*	*	*	/	*	X

Hank is demonstrating difficulties in social/community building skills. His strength is in hands-on activities.

Kelly is demonstrating weaknesses in written language and science concepts.

Maddie is not displaying social/community skills in this setting, additional support (TIER 2) will be needed.

Data has not been collected on blank rows.

Many of the children are demonstrating difficulty with recording findings and representing change.

References Guidance for ELCS Implementation ODE 2005, rev. 2006 © UD 2008

Gifted Children

Children who have been identified as gifted, or just high functioning compared to their peers, will also benefit from the inquiry-based, integrated curriculum offered within *ACCESS*. Intentional planning and teaching provides children with experiences at their level of development. Just like working with a lower functioning child, teachers working with a gifted child intentionally plan ways for that child to expand his/her natural curiosity regarding the topic of study. The planning of investigations and the learning experiences that support the investigation within the *ACCESS*, provides for a range of involvement that invites children to enter and participate at their level.

Authenticity and Misconceptions

Many teachers in preschool and primary classrooms provide activities for children to do as part of the "theme" of the week. These often include art projects to address fine motor, language or cognitive skills but also may include misperceptions about the world. For example, in the picture that follows, the child is tearing paper to cover an apple with a cartoon worm in the center of an apple. Through scientific investigations, the children will know that worms don't eat apples, but instead get their nutrients from the soil as the apple decays. The child with exceptionalities may not understand the difference between fact and fiction and may continue to have the misperception that worms eat their way through an apple.

ACCESS emphasizes focusing on authentic content knowledge with the children engaged in the research to find the answers to questions. Children with exceptionalities are able to participate in this research as well through picture books or Internet sites designed for children. While working with their peers or an adult in the classroom, children with exceptionalities can learn the difference between fact and fantasy and also gain knowledge on the topic being studied.

Chapter Summary

For those of us who are engaged in developmentally appropriate practice, meeting the needs of individual children is what we do every day. Developmentally appropriate practice requires that we understand developmental skills that are typical for the chronological age of the children whom we are caring for and educating. It also focuses on the interests, developmental skills and areas of need for each child. We are used to making decisions, planning experiences and staging environments that support individual children. When working with typically developing children, these supports are often referred to as scaffolding. Once a child has an identified disability, the term changes to modifications and adaptations. Regardless of the language used, the outcome is the same. Effective early childhood teachers meet the needs of the individual children with whom they work.

ACCESS Steps to Success:
Including Children with Exceptionalities

1. Include IFSP or IEP goals and/or objectives on *ACCESS* data collection sheets. When developing an investigation and determining the standards to be addressed in the investigation, IEP goals can be reviewed in the same way. See Figure 7-2 for a sample data sheet.

Figure 7-2 **Observational Check sheet with IEP Goals (OCs)   Topic: Water**

Indicator	Sally	Samantha	Juan	Carlos	Danielle	Logan	Sarah
Begins to use terms to compare the attributes of objects (MII4)							
Measures length and volume using non-standard units of measure (MII6)							
Sorts, orders, and classifies objects by one attribute (MIV1)							
Touches objects and says the number names when counting in the context of daily activities and play (MI2)							
Uses one or more of the senses to observe and learn about objects, organisms and phenomena for a purpose (SV5)							
Participates in simple, spontaneous scientific explorations with others (SVI3)							
Offers ideas and explanations of objects, organisms and phenomena which may be correct or incorrect (SVI1)							
Explores and compares materials that provide many different sensory experiences (SIII2)							

Identifies common needs of familiar living things (SII1)								
Identifies the intended purpose of familiar tools (SIV1)								
Demonstrates cooperative behaviors, such as helping, turn taking, sharing, comforting, and compromising (SSVI1)								
IEP Goals								
Will improve fine motor skills by participating in classroom activities: pour, stir, draw, paint, cut	▨			▨	▨	▨		▨
Will ask questions about objects, organisms and events in their environment			▨	▨	▨	▨		▨
Will sit with a small group (less than six) for up to five minutes with no more than two verbal prompts	▨		▨	▨				▨
Notes:								

References *Guidance for ELCS Implementation ODE 2005, rev. 2006* © UD 2008

2. Schedule data collection so all adults in the room know when and how to take data. One teacher should be scheduled by task and day so each person knows what she is to do with the children and which data to collect.

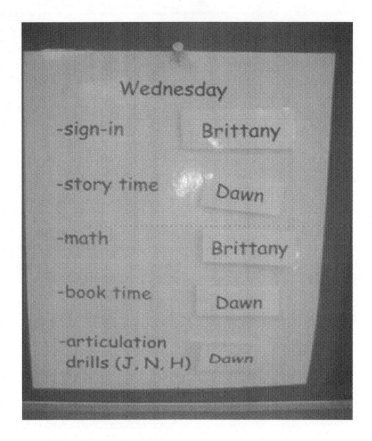

3. Look at both early learning content standards and IEP goals when planning an investigation to see which could be addressed by the planned activity. Develop a data sheet of the standards and goals and have it within easy reach as the children engage in the experiences.

4. Provide all levels of "research" materials. Some children may be able to read text; others may need to look at pictures to discover answers to their questions. But *ACCESS* believes in all children participating to the best of their ability and the need for teachers/staff to be creative in including all children.

5. Develop materials to help children achieve the desired results in simple steps. Below is a picture of sieves that were made from screen material which naturally separated the rocks as each sieve was lifted off the top. The children could then compare what was left on each sieve, documenting though pictures, words, and communicating with an adult or each other that the materials left on each sieve were progressively smaller.

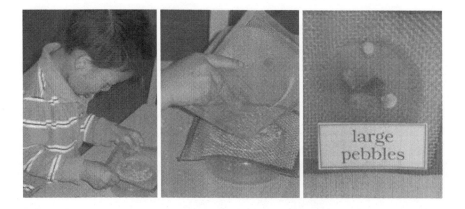

References

Bredekamp, S. (1993). The relationship between early childhood education and early childhood special education: Healthy marriage or family feud? *Topics in Early childhood Special Education, 13*(3), 258-273).

Brenneman, K., Stevenson-Boyd, & Frede, E. C. (2009). Math and Science in Preschool: Policies and Practice. *Preschool Policy Brief,* 19. Rutgers University: National Institute for Early Education Research.

Childress, D. C. (2004). Special instruction and natural environments: Best practices in early intervention. *Infants and Young Children, 17*(2), 162-170.

Council for Exceptional Children. (2008). *Responsiveness to Intervention: A Collection of Articles from TEACHING Exceptional Children.* Arlington, VA: CEC.

Frank Porter Graham Child Development Institute. (2004). *Carolina Curriculum for Preschoolers with Special Needs,* (2nd ed.). Retrieved from *www.fpg.unc.edu.*

High Scope Curriculum. Retrieved from *http://www.highscope.org.*

LaRocque, M., & Darling, S. M. (2008). *Blended curriculum in the inclusive k-3 classroom: Teaching all young children.* Boston, MA: Pearson Publishing.

Merriam, S. B. & Caffarella, R. S. (1999). *Learning in adulthood: A comprehensive guide* (2ed). San Francisco, CA: Jossey-Bass Publishers.

Neisworth, J. T., & Bagnato, S. J. (2005). DEC Recommended Practices: Assessment. In *DEC Recommended Practices: A Comprehensive Guide for Practical Application in Early Intervention/Early Childhood Special Education.* Missoula, MT: Division for Early Childhood.

Sandell, S., Hemmeter, M. L., Smith, B. J., & McLean, M. E. (2005). *DEC Recommended Practices: A Comprehensive Guide for Practical Application in Early Intervention/Early Childhood Special Education.* Missoula, MT: Division for Early Childhood.

Trivette, C. M., & Dunst, C. J. (2005) DEC Recommended Practices: Family-Based Practices. In *DEC Recommended Practices: A Comprehensive Guide for Practical Application in Early Intervention/Early Childhood Special Education.* Missoula, MT: Division for Early Childhood.

Wolery, M. (2005). DEC Recommended Practices: Child-Focused Practices. In *DEC Recommended Practices: A Comprehensive Guide for Practical Application in Early Intervention/Early Childhood Special Education.* Missoula, MT: Division for Early Childhood.

8

ACCESS Steps to Success

This final chapter serves as a quick reference guide for teachers, principals, program directors and curriculum specialists who are interested in a step by step process for implementing *ACCESS*. The Steps to Success that are included at the end of each chapter are listed here as a quick reference. Other formats of this quick guide and additional resources for implementing *ACCESS* can be found at www.accesscurriculum.com.

A. *Assessment Supported Practice*

Designing an Assessment System

1. Preferably before the school year begins, the teaching team identifies assessment practices that currently exist and determines the aspects of the practices that should become part of an intentional assessment system.
2. During the program evaluation process, the team identifies useful assessment data that has been collected using existing strategies. How well can these data inform instructional decisions, document child progress, and identify the interest of the children?
3. The team discusses assessment needs and preferences including how to:
    a. document child progress
    b. inform instructional decision-making
    c. document the interest of children
    d. conduct ongoing program evaluation
4. The team considers the classroom's daily routines and identifies opportunities for documenting developmental skills or early learning content standards.

5. The team considers data collection strategies including the tools provided in the *ACCESS* collection available at *www.accesscurriculum.com* and decides which tools meet the needs of the team, or if they need to modify one of the tools to fit their needs.
6. The teaching team determines the screening tool or tools to be used as children enter the program.
7. The teaching team determines who, where, when and how data will be collected.

Getting to Know Children and Families

1. The teaching team examines data that has been shared about incoming children by families, previous teachers/caregivers, and medical and school records.
2. The teaching team identifies information that still needs to be collected and selects and/or modifies tools from the *ACCESS* collection or creates their own.
3. The team screens the children. NOTE: Screening data is not used to exclude children from the program but rather as a means of informing instructional decisions.
4. The team gathers information from the family through a detailed application, introductory survey, center-based intake interview and/or home-based intake interview.

Compiling Data

1. The team compiles initial data about children using either the hard copy or electronic version of the *ACCESS* Class Tracking Sheets (ACTS) available in the *ACCESS* collection at *www.accesscurriculum.com*.
2. As new data is collected, the team updates the ACTS to reflect current information on the progress and interests of children.

Analyzing and Reflecting on Data

1. The team meets weekly to discuss assessment data as part of the instructional planning process.
2. The team uses data to make instructional decisions, to track progress of individual children and the class as a whole, to identify the interests of children and to evaluate program effectiveness.
3. The team determines what data needs to be collected in the future and adds or deletes tools as needed.

4. The team reflects on data collection processes and adjusts who, when, where, and how data is being collected as needed.

Sharing Progress with Families

1. The team shares information about child progress and interests with families using classroom-based or electronic portfolios, document boards, informal conversation, and formal conferences during quarterly progress report meetings.
2. The team determines how social media and web sites might be used to facilitate information sharing with families. See *www. accesscurriculum.com* for social media safety information.
3. The team determines an ongoing process to share important program philosophies and early childhood research-based practice with families. For example:
   a. Kindergarten readiness is not an event but rather a process that begins in utero.
   b. Developmentally appropriate and play-based practice is the best way to grow the brain and get children ready for kindergarten and later school success.

The Transition Process

1. The team develops a transition process that facilitates information sharing with programs that are receiving children from your program.
2. The team selects, revises or develops transition documents that share information with programs that are receiving children from the program.
3. The team identifies and/or plans opportunities to visit and/or learn about program options so that families can make informed decisions.

B. Child-Centered Practice

Teachers and teaching teams:

1. Conduct a self-assessment of the environment using the *Infant Toddler Environment Rating Scale—Revised* (ITERS-R) (Harms,T., Clifford, R.M., & Cryer, D., 2006); the *Early Childhood Environment Rating Scale-Revised* (ECERS-R) (Clifford, R.M., Cryer, D., & Harms, T, 2004); or the *Classroom Environment Self-Assessment:*

Kindergarten-Primary (CESA: K-P) (Adams, Baldwin, Comingore and Kelly, 2013, p.) and identify areas of strength and goals for the classroom environment.

2. Become familiar with age appropriate development of the children in your classroom.
3. Get to know the families of the children and gather information about family culture that will inform child centered experiences.
4. Observe children to become familiar with their individual strengths, needs and interest.
5. Use the "Assessment of Play" checklist to gain understanding of the types of social and cognitive play present in the classroom. Reevaluate play and adjust the environment throughout the year.
6. Arrange your classroom considering the needs of your children and the results of the self-assessment of your environment. Reevaluate and adjust the environment to support development and learning throughout the year.
7. Select authentic materials that will support exploration, inquiry, language and concept development and play.
8. Place materials in the classroom in such a way that they are highlighted and provide cues for appropriate storage.
9. Rotate materials to reflect the current curriculum and store unused materials out of site to reduce visual clutter.
10. Support children's play without directing it.
11. Be intentional with teacher directed experiences.
12. Analyze and interpret assessment data/documentation when planning experiences that meet the children's learning and developmental needs.
13. Incorporate the interests of children as well as their questions in classroom experiences.

C. Emergent Negotiated Curriculum

ACCESS Steps to Success: Emergent Negotiated Curriculum

1. Before the year begins, become familiar with the investigations the children engaged in during the previous year. If possible talk with last year's teachers to discover areas of untapped interest.
2. Review student portfolios and other assessment data that can inform your understanding of what the children are ready to work on next.
3. Refresh your understanding of the learning and development standards for the age level of your children and review the concepts and skills that

the children are likely to be working on. Keep in mind that infants and toddler tend to focus more on developmental skills and, as children become older, the amount of focus on academic content increases. Regardless of age, a challenging curriculum includes developmental skills which cannot be overlooked even with 4th and 5th graders.

4. Survey families to determine their interests, expertise and willingness to participate in the classroom.

5. Start out the year with a range of authentic materials that could inspire interest. Select materials that will attract children and encourage them to be engaged.

6. Once a topic begins to emerge, add related materials to the environment to verify the children's level of interest as well as the specific aspect of the topic that they are most interested in.

7. Continue to observe children to follow their lead to the next aspect of the investigation. Document their understandings.

D. Science and Inquiry

To support children's scientific inquiry, teachers and teaching teams should:

1. Observe children's knowledge, experiences, and interests when selecting a topic for investigation.

2. Select a science topic for investigation that provides opportunities for use of inquiry and the science processes, naturally integrates other content areas and developmental domains, is personally meaningful and social relevant for children, and provides opportunities to interact with authentic, engaging materials.

3. Develop your own science content knowledge pertinent to the selected topic by engaging in professional development through workshops, blogs and research.

4. Use the science concept planner to design experience for your children that will allow them to investigate the topic.

5. Gather developmentally appropriate, multisensory, authentic materials that can be utilized throughout your classroom and outdoor environment to stimulate children's interest, questioning, and problem solving related to the topic.

6. Gather high quality, developmentally appropriate, engaging print materials, including fiction and non-fiction books which children will find interesting and useful, either on their own or with adult support.

7. Allow time in your classroom for the topic to evolve. Guide student questions, experiences, interests and investigations into relevant questions by providing multiple experiences to investigate the topic.

E. Standards Integrated

To integrate standards, teachers:

1. Plan and stage environments to inspire young children to play, to think and to engage in inquiry.
2. Observe children to determine areas of interest.
3. Analyze possible topics for investigation ensuring that they are worthy of study, reflect the interests of children and are broad enough to support learning and development.
4. Brainstorm to complete a science concept planner, or learning experience planner if working with infants and/or toddlers.
5. Connect curriculum in meaningful ways by selecting content standards from several disciplines and developmental domains, making sure to include children's IEP goals. Infant and toddler teachers should focus on developmental skills.
6. Create and use authentic assessment tools to add data to the ACTS.
7. Plan future investigations and learning experiences around assessment results, integrating standards and developmental skills across the curriculum.

F. Including Children with Exceptionalities

To ensure the inclusion of children with exceptionalities, teachers and teams should:

1. Include IFSP or IEP goals and/or objectives on *ACCESS* data collection sheets. When developing an investigation and determining the standards to be addressed in the investigation, IEP goals can be reviewed in the same way.
2. Schedule data collection so all adults in the room know when and how to take data. One teacher should be scheduled by task and day so each person knows what she is to do with the children and which data to collect;

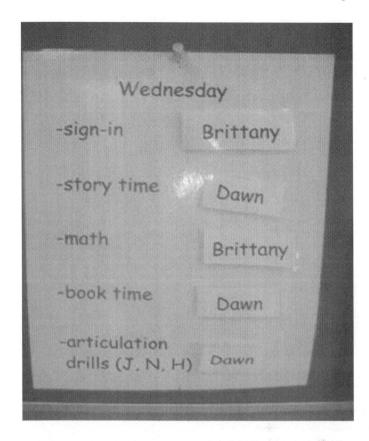

3. Look at both early learning and development standards as well as IEP goals when planning an investigation to see which could be addressed by the planned activity. Develop a data sheet of the standards and goals and have it within easy reach as the children engage in the experiences;

4. Provide all levels of "research" materials. Some children may be able to read text. Others may need to look at pictures to discover answers to their questions. But *ACCESS* believes in all children participating to the best of their ability and the need for teachers/staff to be creative in including all children;

5. Develop materials to help children achieve the desired results in simple steps.

41925728R00140

Made in the USA
Lexington, KY
01 June 2015